W9-CHU-248

For Elena Wilson

with many thanks to Nathalie Goodwin for her moral support and constant encouragement during the writing of these notebooks.

# American Notebooks
# A Writer's Journey

Marie-Claire Blais

Translated by

Linda Gaboriau

Talonbooks

Published with the assistance of the Canada Council.

*Talonbooks*
*#104—3100 Production Way*
*Burnaby, British Columbia, Canada V5A 4R4*

Typeset in Bembo and Nuptial Script and printed and bound in Canada by Hignell Printing Ltd.

First Printing: September 1996

**Canadian Cataloguing in Publication Data**

Blais, Marie-Claire, 1939–
    [Parcours d'un écrivain. English]
    American notebooks

    Translation of: Parcours d'un écrivain.
    ISBN 0-88922-358-0

    I. Title. II. Title: Parcours d'un écrivain. English.
PS8503.L33Z5313 1996        C844'.54        C96-910278-X
PQ3919.B6Z47213 1996

# Notebook 1

*S**pring is exploding** in the streets of Montreal when I meet Edmund and Elena Wilson (Edmund is in touch with some Québécois authors) in one of the bars at the Ritz Carlton, one day in <u>May 1963.</u> Both of them impress me with their distinguished poise, their affable smiles, their way of dressing, English clothes in subtle hues, in which they both seem so comfortable, as if they'd just returned from a brisk walk—although Edmund is wearing a beige scarf around his neck and his shirt is unbuttoned, his tie loosened beneath the lapel of his jacket.

Against the dark blue velvet wallpaper, they graciously match the decor of the hotel, with its subdued lighting on this late afternoon. I worry, as I listen to them talk about their house in Wellfleet on Cape Cod (where Elena invites me to join her in the fall, when she'll be alone and missing her daughter Helen who will soon be leaving to study in Switzerland), about my unkempt appearance in the oversized sweater I threw over my shoulders as I left my room on Prince Arthur Street where I live with some students from McGill.

The Hungarian woman who runs our boarding house has strict principles, forbidding the women students to receive men at night, and screening our phone calls as well. Yet she's the one who, like a good fairy, comes knocking at my door to tell me that I received the fellowship from the John Simon Guggenheim Memorial Foundation; she also tells me that Edmund and Elena are expecting me at five o'clock in one of the lounges at the Ritz where I'll find my shyness so painful in my faltering expression of gratitude, over a glass of whiskey. Edmund and Elena, who appear to understand everything, who have read everything and can discuss everything, from music to foreign literature, seem to have descended from those Olympian regions where one can only admire them from afar with occasional fits of anger.

What can they know, I think, about the apprenticeship of a young writer, about the arduous world of work, about difficult living conditions—although these difficulties have lessened for me recently, thanks to Louise Myette who has initiated me to paleography at the Montreal Courthouse where she is a pillar of competence—am I not quickly offended by reactions I would consider petty today? So, I think, Edmund and Elena's daughter Helen (who several years later will earn a fine reputation as a painter in New York, among the painters of her generation) is about to go study in Switzerland, at age fourteen, the age when others are subjected to bitter and repulsive working conditions, in stores, evenings after school, or when they have to drop out of school to help their families, in those factories where they are paid less than a dollar an hour.

What world of flagrant injustice am I about to enter? Is the writer's tool his or her indifference, her impermeability to others, or her excessive sensitivity subjected to every experience? But Edmund whom, from the first day we met, I compare to the powerful (and avuncular) British head of state, Winston Churchill, quickly revives my faith in the future when he says, with a wry twinkle in his eye: "You'll see, this difficult period is over... all you'll have to do for a year in the States is write in peace..." Together we choose the city of Cambridge, near Boston, a few hours from Wellfleet on the Atlantic coast.

Elena is stunningly beautiful, although her appeal is in no way conventional, with her strong, irregular features, her high cheekbones that seem permanently flushed by the cold (Elena enjoys invigorating sports and tells me she swims every day until late November in the icy ocean). Her smile, when she's annoyed, is drawn taut over magnificent, slightly prominent white teeth; she sometimes appears plagued by inner tensions, by some obscure duty of a seemingly religious nature (speaking of her friend, the poet Auden, Elena will call him a saint; she will often express belief in the role of involuntary and secular sainthood when speaking of Martin Luther King; she also believes in the absolute obedience a woman owes to the man she loves—this will be the subject of a prolonged altercation between her and me during my first visit in the fall of 1963); but that day, in the lounge of the Ritz Carlton, Elena has the dignity of one of Thomas Mann's heroines, preserving in her mystery the secrets of an old aristocratic Europe, she who since her exile from Germany and a past heavy with sorrow, has sought in North America the site of her homeland, not knowing whether she can truly find here, among these puritans of another language, the homeland that was lost, along with so many of its children.

Most of all I'm struck by Elena's eyes that captivate everyone who looks into them and never forgets them: they are a deep, dark blue, they sparkle with a light that can suddenly turn cold, metallic, and their gentleness is hermetic.

In the bar at the Ritz Carlton, the three of us raise our glasses "to the new life about to begin in Cambridge."

# Notebook 2

*June 1963*: later that year a great American president will be assassinated, with the nascent war in Vietnam, we will all become witnesses, on television and in the newspapers, to an era of massacres, interrupted occasionally by movements of collective awareness that will change the world. For the very first time on television, we'll see a young black woman, followed by the National Guard, walk through the gates of a white university, racial segregation will be attacked, denounced—with hatred, pain, righteous anger, peacefully too—and we will see black and white militants, the martyrs of this conflict, lose their lives in cities in the South of the United States, martyrs who continue to fall in the streets of Los Angeles and Toronto today, in this fight for the civil rights of Blacks, rights not yet won even now. But in June 1963, the city of Cambridge, Massachusetts where we arrive by car one sunny afternoon is calm, with its dreamy students lying on the lawns of the Harvard University campus. The recipient of a Guggenheim fellowship, I have to spend a year in the United States writing a book; I chose Cambridge because I have friends who live there, but they are writers whose maturity, formidable body of work and fame intimidate me and I'm afraid to meet them or see them again. Louise and Françoise who are going to spend their vacation in

Provincetown, have been kind enough to drive me to Cambridge and help me with my modest move to the States; I have brought only the few essential things that constituted my belongings at the time: a card table, foldable and austere, to write on, a chair, a pink plastic radio and the most precious of my tools, a portable typewriter. Within an hour, we've rented a basement apartment for a hundred dollars a month, in the black neighbourhood near Cambridge. It's in a huge grey, dilapidated building inhabited by students from around the world; in the dark corridor to my apartment, I notice that some of the mail-boxes have been broken into and many of the windows in the building have been shattered. It's my first day in Cambridge; when my friends leave for Provincetown, my heart is heavy as I walk alone towards the university campus, and I wonder why I decided to live in this rather cold, haughty city where I don't yet dare speak to anyone, except my landlord, a rude man, hostile to foreigners. But it's a beautiful June day, and in the bookstores on Brattle Street, young people dressed in their jeans and corduroy pants stand crowded together, reading; they're everywhere, in the bookstores, in the entrances to the movie houses, in the cafés, in the bars where I'll often hear them laughing and talking late into the night. Silent or noisy, they feel at home in this city conceived for them. They all carry their books in a backpack, or in a red canvas bag with a yellow strap slung over their shoulders, into which they throw the books collected during the day, at the university library—where Edmund Wilson will kindly take me for the first time—or at the countless bookstores where, without buying a thing, anyone can spend hours reading the works of Walt Whitman, Herman Melville, Henry James; that's where I discover, standing among the others in front of the shelves of books we eye greedily as we read, Mary McCarthy, the poets Elizabeth Bishop and Marianne Moore, whose brief presence in my life several years later, in the company of friends, will leave a lasting impression. These writers I read in the newness of a language other than my own—a language I'm just learning during these hot June days spent wandering around the city, alone, aware of my uneasiness, my strangeness in this place—these writers make me realize that a bit of my spiritual home awaits me here, in their company. But I have to escape the dark, sordid room, with the window I can't close that lets in the rain, the snow, and the white cat who comes to visit whenever he's hungry. It's during these June days when I'm already fighting a keen desire to return home, to be with my friends— during this period of prolonged, uneasy idleness when I don't even dare open a bank account, speak to the grocer, express myself awkwardly in a language I hardly speak—that my life is suddenly transformed by the purchase of a bicycle. (In all I'll own three bicycles, two of which are stolen within a few days, although I chain them at night to a tree I can see from my window; all that will eventually remain of the third is two wheels with the tires torn off in the courtyard behind my building.) For it's on this bicycle that I discover the city, its nonchalance on Sunday afternoon along the banks of the Charles River, its cheerful families having lunch on the bank of the river with their dogs, and, in their racing shells, the very young boys dressed in their white shorts, their red jerseys, rowing with concentrated exuberance, their stiffly held bodies bobbing mechanically over the water. On these splendid Sundays the war preparations are seemingly forgotten; in our city, everyone is lighthearted, enjoying the sensuality of youth, and there are perhaps only a few of us who feel oppressed by the imminent catastrophes casting their shadows.

One evening, while walking side by side with a student from MIT, pushing our bicycles along the flowery walkways of a park, my head brushing the shoulder of this tall athletic boy who is walking beside me, crushing the leaves beneath his wide running shoes (he's one of the runners you see at dawn on the shore of the Charles River), I first experience the shock of what I imagine to be an American insensitivity: but is it really the insensitivity, indifference or ignorance of this boy who is asking me so many questions with such virile confidence, or is it my own shyness that paralyses me in his presence? When I tell him I come from Canada, that I've written several books that have been published in the States, the MIT student replies with a self-satisfied air that I'm very lucky to have a publisher in Boston, because Canada, he adds turning his handsome profile towards me, Canada isn't known in our country, Canada is nothing. Just nothing. In the same imperious tone of voice, he asks, "what would you be without us, nothing, right, nothing?" As I look at him standing there with his hand on the seat of his bicycle, his tall head lifted toward the sky of this starry June night, I know I'll meet many people like him who will overwhelm me with the same lack of sensitivity, the same insolence, and that every one of them will inspire the same fear in me. But then, the next day, or a few days later, there'll be another student who will say, on the same walkway under the trees leading to the university buildings: "I'm seventeen, I'll join the army if I have to... I'll do my duty, but I'd rather not be killed, I'd rather not die..."

# Notebook 3

*D*uring *this scorching summer* of 1963, black youths loot and wreak havoc in the streets of my neighbourhood, not too far from the centre of Cambridge, streets that might resemble those in Harlem with the funereal holes in the windows of the houses, the gaping ruins of storefronts behind heavy iron grating that no longer seems to protect anything; but in these days of race riots throughout the country, the army, the police are patrolling the streets, and I'll often see these teenagers with handcuffs on their wrists, or dispersed during the riots with the humiliating fire hoses, blinded by clouds of tear gas; I'll also see them leaving in police cars for their place of imprisonment, their proud heads hidden under their jackets. The time is fast approaching when some will return as warriors, in these same cities, these same streets where we can hear, with the Black Panthers, the rumbling of the violent black revolution.

That summer, on Brookline Street where I live, a victim like everyone around me of this summer of discontent and fury, I read James Baldwin, Richard Wright, Ralph Ellison, and I become aware of one of the most shameful repressions in history. On our street no one can escape the tremendous anger rocking the country, not even my white cat who prowls freely all night and whose dusty fur I stroke in the morning and who one day will fail to return, because some young vandals kill him for fun under the stairs of a building near mine. Just as those fragile and malleable objects, our bicycles, will be twisted out of shape; sometimes we find them charred, attached to poles along the street like small corpses. The student from a wealthy family who blissfully takes LSD after his courses on the lawn of Harvard Yard, who seems to be slipping innocent lumps of sugar under his tongue, will be robbed in his luxurious room, attacked in the street by gangs; discreetly, for the moment, LSD, the drug of sublime escapism in times of war, is shared among professors and students and people praise the swiftness of this euphoric substance still classified as a pharmaceutical product. Worrying disorders begin to appear among the students; it's not unusual, when a student is on her way home from the movies at night, or from the municipal library that closes late, for a boy to come lunging at her, aggressively pointing the red dagger of his naked sex at her without even seeing her, for LSD has the power to release them all from their chains, rapists or poets; suddenly they are able to write like Keats, even if all one can see of these poems is a few mysterious signs on a blank page, a circle, a square, the shape of a star, like these atrophied signs my friend Jack shows me, near the Charles River; they can kill an entire family in cold blood like the assassin whose picture appeared in the morning paper, or compose the music of John Cage they heard in a concert hall, for in a way this music is them, their discordance in these unsettling years, the years of their youth whose harmony has been shattered. Yes, they are daring and LSD captures the hallucinating colours of their most outrageous dreams of liberation.

Miss B., a pious Irish Catholic who invites me to join her for lunch at one of Cambridge's more elegant restaurants (she is sympathetic to my embarrassment when she sees me searching for my passport at the bottom of the red bag which I too wear over my shoulder, since we must constantly prove that we are over twenty-one to be served a drink in a restaurant, although the students, as soon as they're alone, drink countless beers at their private parties), Miss B., the collar of her stiff dress buttoned up to her chin, tells me: "These young people are going too far... They have no principles in life... This city is a nightmare for people like me who live in urban areas... And yet, we're decent citizens ... And these Blacks, why don't they stay where they belong? They have their own streets, their own neighbourhoods, why do they have to invade ours? Do we really have to share everything with them? Our universities? Our schools?"

From the honest lips of Miss B., this kind and patriotic woman, come these hateful words which suddenly make me mistrust her. Yet she says to me in the words of sincere friendship: "Why are you so afraid to call your American friends?... Your friends will help you, you'll see, Americans are generous... You're so alone, why don't you come to my house next Sunday... We'll have lunch in the garden if the weather is nice..." In her neat garden, like so many gardens in New England, in this garden where a fountain flows near an imposing statue of the Virgin Mary, I have lunch with Miss B., who while picking the tulips she carefully arranges at the foot of the statue, speaks to me of her fervent faith; she says young people are wrong to be atheists who live without God, and what a terrible state the country is in because of these young people and their self-declared liberation which erases all the rules of the past; she is shocked, offended, she is exasperated too because it's late in her life and she no longer hopes to find a husband, but men aren't what they used to be... Her mother nods with approval, thoughtful beneath her trembling chignon. "It's all quite awful," she says, "what's happening to religion, and our country, what will become of our great country, falling prey to vandals?" I think it's during a discussion about sexual freedom that Miss B. suddenly tells me in the same restaurant where she so kindly invited me to lunch a few weeks earlier: "I don't approve of your ideas, I know that's the way your generation thinks, but I don't approve of your way of thinking, so it would be better for us not to see each other again." Yet in this new world, New England, every experience, everything, even this distressing encounter with Miss B. and her racial and religious intolerance, becomes a source of daily discovery, and on the card table in my basement room, the notebooks overflow.

# Notebook 4

*It's a July afternoon*, far from Broadway Street and its ominous prowlers lurking in the doorways of the stores and buildings whose windows have been blackened with hateful slogans. In the parks of Cambridge, people are relaxing, enjoying the peaceful Sunday concert of bells in the neighbourhood churches. This Sunday, I'm sitting on a bench beside Edmund Wilson, who—in his deep voice, softened by long silences, for our conversation is taking place in French, and although he speaks the language perfectly, Edmund sometimes pauses on a word, a phrase, respectfully hesitant— with the breadth of his vast culture, is sketching a detailed portrait of Virginia Woolf, of her life and her work. And I don't dare glance at this man who looks like Winston Churchill, who has such a powerful intellect and physical presence. He also speaks, with the same passionate knowledge, of the works of Zelda Fitzgerald, the poet Edna Saint-Vincent Millay, Gertrude Stein, and he speaks authoritatively of the writers of the new rebellion, whose work I've just read at the Harvard library, as if each one of these admirable women were among his closest friends. This man, blessed with fabulous intuitions, seems to understand the crystal-clear vision of Virginia Woolf who throughout her entire life sought, through the trials and complexity of her art, a revelation which eluded her and for which she had to die. I stare at the blue sky nervously, yet my eyes also linger on the sleeve of the worn tweed jacket Edmund is wearing despite the heat, on his brown shoes, old-fashioned oxfords, with one lace untied. I'd like to ask Edmund why the works of Virginia Woolf, her life for him so full of moral ambiguity, and her refusal to submit to social conventions, seem so familiar to him, but Edmund is an erudite man, the author of some twenty books, the most well-known of which have already appeared in paperback, books that can be found in all the bookstores of Cambridge and that I read standing among the students (*I Thought of Daisy, To the Finland Station, The Wound and the Bow*). Confronted with such erudition, I, whose mind is not yet cultivated, whose literary career is just beginning, must remain silent. But I've already experienced the same irritation or the same discomfort when reading biographies of Simone Weil written by men, I've never liked this proprietorial tone, so rigid and smug, the tone, in the sixties, of male critics or biographers presenting or analysing works written by women. Edmund reminds me that Virginia Woolf wrote an audacious fictional biography, *Orlando*. He tells me I would undoubtedly like this avant-garde biography very much... "Orlando," he explains with a trace of derision in the inflection of his voice, "is a character who travels through time, through history, becoming alternately a man or a woman. The book is all the more surprising because it was written by a woman." I'd seen a picture of Edmund on the cover of one of his books; you could see in the picture, as I can today on this bench in a park in Cambridge, the majesty of Winston Churchill, the same mordant irony in the thin-lipped smile, except that in the picture Edmund is also a jester, a magician, because he's holding a pack of cards; and on this weekend afternoon, I suddenly find myself thinking of the magician in the man. Rather than bore him with my thoughts on Virginia Woolf, overwhelm him with my opinions, or my questions—why does he speak to me of Virginia Woolf, of Gertrude Stein with such a sense of intellectual ownership, why am I shocked by his familiarity with the life and work of Virginia Woolf?—I suggest that he come with me to a puppet show, since he himself stages a puppet show for his grandchildren when they visit him at Christmas.

And so this peaceful day in a Cambridge park comes to end at the theatre, with a puppet show for children. The conversation about Virginia Woolf is postponed: the subject of women's literature, a subject both free and constrained between Edmund and me, will always be tainted by an underlying tension, for I'll always feel as if the great critic is claiming exclusive rights to this treasure that doesn't belong to him. And yet, there are so many hidden affinities between him and Virginia Woolf, and with the fierce and proud soul of Gertrude Stein perhaps even more so. On this Sunday in July, 1963, as I sit on the bench beside Edmund, I'm moved by the greatness of his mind, the subtlety of his perceptions, perhaps I'm blinded by my anger, my revolt, because I know that he studied at a prestigious private university for men only, while Virginia Woolf, born into the erudite circle of philosophers her father frequented, never had a right to such studies, to this intellectual fulfillment. But perhaps the vision of a "luminous halo" surrounding the awareness that guides us from life to death could only be granted to one woman, to Virginia Woolf, in the heroism of her mental isolation, the isolation from which, she says, we must escape...

# Notebook 5

*A golden light* bathes the banks of the Charles River while the oarsmen row in their white shorts; the leaves on the trees have begun to turn red along the prosperous avenues of Boston, between the quaint commercial buildings the incendiary rage of the children of the ghetto has not yet reduced to flames, as it does every day in my neighbourhood, near Cambridge. It's August, 1963 and I am finally emerging from the solitude of my room, after several reclusive months spent on a novel whose subject is passion, the always peculiar relationship between a man and a woman, and after the stolen bicycle incident which I relate to a close friend who writes back with the masculine authority I'd forgotten, so distant: "This kind of thing only happens to women... It's takes someone clumsy like you, or too naive with people, so trusting you attract this kind of trouble..." And so begins my story about thwarted passion or ambivalence, the uncertainty of male-female relationships which has always haunted me. I call the friends whose number Edmund Wilson kindly gave me, that bright Sunday afternoon in July, on the bench, in the park in Cambridge. And now, in late August, the respite, the delight of hearing French spoken in this English-speaking world so smug in its religious and moral values, even more withdrawn and retiring at this time of the year when the university session is about to resume. Professor Suzanne P., here from France to teach modern French literature at Harvard, invites me to her home with its white walls, her children, their cats and dogs, the boisterous family running barefoot down the stairs and over the white wool carpets, in the rays of sunlight streaming through the bay window onto these small fragile and joyous bodies. Suddenly their mother says sternly they must get ready for dinner before their father comes home, get dressed, and washed, and most of all they must be quiet at the table and keep their animals silently hidden under their chairs.

As we sit bathed in light, in the last glow before autumn of the hot summer sun caressing our hair, and as the red roses open in a vase on the white tablecloth, Suzanne explains her approach to teaching the existentialist writers, from Gabriel Marcel to Jean-Paul Sartre and Simone de Beauvoir. She admits that she fears for her students; these young Americans will soon face serious decisions about their future, several have expressed the desire to become conscientious objectors if war is declared. All this time, the children are playing under the table with their favourite animals.

What attracts me so spontaneously to Suzanne and her family that day is not so much the childhood paradise she has managed to create around those she loves, it's also the delightful lure of Provence I hear in her accent, and the colourful warmth of the way she speaks French. And Suzanne is also interested in our literature, and in Edmund's book, (*O Canada, An American Note on Canadian Culture*) where he strives to unite our two separate cultures, estranged from each other during the nebulous period of the sixties, through his subtle interpretation of writers of both languages. The writers studied include Morley Callaghan, Hugh MacLennan, as well as Anne Hébert, Roger Lemelin, André Langevin.

Twenty years later, at a book signing at Schoenhof's International Bookstore in Cambridge where they've always supported French-language writers from Québec, I'll see Suzanne P., her husband Peter, the children who are now at university themselves, the whole blossoming family so interested in our books and writers, and Suzanne will say to me in her same delicious accent: "There are no longer any children under the table, one of the girls is studying to be a doctor... I don't know about the other yet... but at home, we're still interested in your writers... at Harvard, we know Anne Hébert's work, Antonine Maillet, Michel Tremblay, Réjean Ducharme... some day, we'd like to host more of your writers here..." I'll hear this confident and stimulating comment often, in American universities during reading tours, alone or with other writers. Occasionally there'll be an ardent admirer of Victor-Lévy Beaulieu who (having heard him read at one of these universities) will speak to me in French about his books, and the same sensation of precarious but comforting pleasure will fill me again, as it did in Suzanne's house with the white walls and the children, in August, 1963 with the sun's brilliant rays beating down on us through the bay window. To relish some thirty years later, the delight and the wonder of hearing the voice of our poets or people speaking about them abroad with the limpid precision of the French language might seem trite when one thinks that we are daily witnesses to the worst horrors of our era, and the persistence of war and famine that give our helpless eyes, our paralysed consciences no respite. Yet isn't such frail delight all that remains?

# Notebook 6

*I*n the early fall of 1963, while student unrest dominates the Harvard campus—the Vietnam War is about to break out, dividing the entire country—once again I have the pleasure of hearing French spoken, this time with the slightly sing-song brusqueness of a New England accent, while visiting Maud Morgan's studio on Howland Street, in a respectable neighbourhood of Cambridge where there is a row of pretty green-painted houses set among cedars, with their fenced-in gardens. These visits rekindle my fascination for American non-figurative painting which, in Maud's stunning paintings, with their fertile abstract shapes dripping red and gold, unbridled yet rigorously contained in a miraculous explosion, precedes the advent of pop art, and soon thereafter, with the tumultuous Andy Warhol and his powerful social denunciations, of a school of painting blatant in its treatment of current events and everyday life that one wonders whether it isn't almost too real an image of what we have become in the thrall of the products we consume. Isn't the Campbell soup can there in our inner eye, hasn't it invaded our imaginations, like the haunting face of Marilyn Monroe whose eyes seem blind to the tragedy endlessly multiplied (for there will be at least one hundred images representing with the same precision this face masked with a false smile, with the feigned resignation of a woman who is the only one to know the violent end destiny holds in store for her.)

Maud is a tall energetic woman with white hair: she lives alone, although she often sees her son and her daughter to whom she feels very close; at nearly fifty years old, she says with her wry sense of humour that she is trying to assert her right to autonomy both as a person and an artist. As I look at her paintings in a studio where the wide windowpanes reflect the already cold blue of an autumn sky, standing there among the white unfinished canvasses that a stroke of her brush has flooded with a splash of luminous shapes that glow in the middle of the canvas, in contrast with the white, a burst of torrid yellow, Maud tells me that she works on several paintings at a time every day. I don't yet realize that Maud, who, thirty years later, continues to paint and exhibit around the world, embodies prophetically for me all the women artists, painters, engravers, sculptors, whom I will soon meet in the United States, Canada, and France, and who, like Maud, will all defend their art with the same integrity and the same fierce autonomy.

Several years later in New York, I'll see paintings by Jackson Pollock, Gorky and Hans Hoffman, and their blurring of colour and shape, their poignant expression of our tormented times, and the same profusion of splashes scratched, structured, torn from the chaos of raw material, will remind me of Maud and her bold rupture with traditional art; these paintings will make me believe in the influence of painting on writing, in the ability of one art to colour another by injecting itself, as when Proust describes a ray of yellow light on a wall, when he refines with his own perceptions a painting by Vermeer or a portrait by Rembrandt which imperceptibly becomes a portrait of the writer himself.

As anger simmers on university campuses, and the fear of war is on everyone's lips, art is also provocative and its aggressive shockwaves are beneficial; on Brattle Street in Cambridge, people are lining up to see films by Godard, Buñuel. Soon they'll be storming the galleries to see paintings by Andy Warhol (at the time he looks like a dreamy little boy, harmless beneath his blond hair with the perennial lock over an anxious eye) and by Roy Lichtenstein whose paintings shout the decline of industrial society. One of the Warhol paintings will weigh on my memory for years. The canvas contains only one object, as if the painter had photographed it in the dark or meticulously drawn it with a black pencil: an electric chair, empty, waiting. In 1963, we have just abolished the death penalty in Canada. In the United States, capital punishment still exists, although on all the university campuses from Harvard to Berkeley, students continue to oppose it vigorously. Andy Warhol and Jackson Pollock, who have invaded the New York art galleries like the barbarians of a new school of painting, these two artists who shock the critics, who create such a fuss, will both die in solitary catastrophes of which we know very little, except that one of them was sick and the other given to driving too fast on the highways where he will perish in an accident.

One evening in September 1992, I hear Maud's voice on the phone, in the somewhat chilly country house where I've taken refuge this season, rarely seeing my friends; it's an elderly voice I don't recognize at first, a broken voice, that of a very old woman. I learn that she is still painting and exhibiting work, and that she is writing her autobiography. I hadn't heard Maud's voice since that visit to her studio in the fall of 1963, but as I listen to it, I can still see her paintings intact in the studio on Howland Street in Cambridge, and the hand which, with a broad stroke of the brush, projected onto the canvas those liquid splashes of colour that captured the sun's glow...

# Notebook 7

*These autumn evenings,* when the air is still mild, the black youths loiter in the streets of Cambridge, hands in their pockets, caps down over their eyes. Yet they jump at the slightest noise, in the idleness of the fear that leads them to the foul-smelling shadows of the ghetto's alleyways, amidst the garbage pails where the rats scrounge. They exchange hard drugs—mescaline, heroin—to which, at age thirteen, they have already developed a weary, disillusioned addiction. The poignant death of their souls can sometimes be seen in their eyes, yet they're still young, they like to play, to wrestle, to stroll in gangs at night by the stores locked behind their metal gratings and walls of wrought iron; that's where the older teenagers stop to watch the blue television screen where they see their pacifist leaders and brothers (although the ideology of non-violence does not appeal to these children who experienced very early the violent oppression of the whites) exhorting the politicians to take urgent, immediate non-violent action to ensure the integration of Blacks into American society. On Broadway Street, these teenagers standing at the store windows, mesmerized by the eloquent figures speaking to them from a distant blue screen, listen and watch, with an intensity that vies with disenchantment, the gentle preacher named Martin Luther King, whose words, like those of a poet, overflow with images, metaphors, cautious advice and also with an unfaltering tenderness, for one day all men will be brothers, they hear, and the integration of Blacks will take place peacefully, through non-violence and legislative reform. The young people also watch the ascetic Malcolm X, with the solemn face of an intellectual framed by small glasses; soon they will also see the writer James Baldwin. All of these men will reclaim their African heritage which has been assaulted, stolen—they will all reclaim, sometimes spilling their blood for it, their freedom, the innocence of a freedom betrayed century after century. These young people who are hunted by the police, who have already looted the streets of their cities, who will be locked up in penitentiaries for drug dealing, listen and they watch, and their eyes grow big with hope. Could it be true? Could there be a better future for them? In Harvard Yard, on the banks of the Charles River, where, unfortunately for him, my friend Jack pursues his experiments with hallucinogenic drugs, the evangelical message of Martin Luther King is also heard and listened to; through the din of the riots, the wisdom of this message sounds like the murmur of an ocean growing calmer. Many students, like Jack, participate in the March on Washington and share the idealism, the humanism of the great Baptist preacher, momentarily abandoning their Acid and LSD. This fall, I too stand among the spectators of the blue screen in store windows when I go out in the evening—my modest means don't allow me to purchase a television set. The faces of Martin Luther King, Malcolm X have invaded the silence of my room, along with the power of their words. On my work table, the fictionalized study of the complex relationship between man and woman has been forgotten for the time being. I observe with fervent interest the events all around me, in my neighbourhood, here in the black community in which I live, and in my work cell where a visitor has yet to set foot, my solitude takes on new meaning. Quite awkwardly still, I try to describe in a new novel about social differences, what I've seen in Québec society that might be comparable to the situation of the Blacks, what still disturbs me, even from abroad—the world of factories where I saw so many young lives wither, fade forever. (This book about working-class life that would take so long to write would become, over the years and through several versions, *The Manuscripts of Pauline Archange*.) The basis for the book is here, in these notebooks piled up on the card table brought to Cambridge, but I don't yet know what form the book will take. I am overcome by suffocating feelings of impotence and I often flee my work table and my uncomfortable chair, for a bicycle ride with Jack or one of my other student friends. It's hard to believe, given my constant need for distraction, that one day I'll become a captive of this art, the art of shedding light on chaos.

The words that come to mind to describe the humiliation of one social class by another (in the late fifties in Québec, where one class clearly dominated another, that of the bosses over the workers who were without protection and even more degraded by a despotic man in power) are bleak words; they have the very tone of the sullen pain I feel.

I wonder what has become of all those young girls, all those young boys, fifteen, sixteen years old, working in the grey factories filled with poisonous fumes from eight in the morning until eight at night. In the subway stations when I see the back of a black man bent over the white man's shoes that he's shining, they are the ones I think of, those young girls, those boys from a race of slaves, at home, in my own country.

# Notebook 8

*I*t's a brilliant October day, full of the luminosity that late summer brings to Cape Cod, and a rosy light bathes the fields, the apple trees, behind Edmund and Elena Wilson's house in Wellfleet where I am spending several days. One can see, from the main road that leads to the vast beaches of Truro, to the dunes of Provincetown overlooking the sea, the white clapboard house (and the lower adjoining house, the children's house they so generously offer to the numerous writers who come here to write). It's a bare house, austere, where the shutters are closed in the evening, around the time the old dog scratches at the door to come in: but today, we're savouring the waning summer, the shutters, like the blue curtains behind them, are blowing in the gentle wind off the water and the old dog is sleeping under a tree.

In this house where I'm alone with Elena (her daughter Helen, whom she adores, has just left for Europe, Edmund has withdrawn to his family home far from everyone to finish a book), I can hear the shuffling of our steps on the varnished wood floor in this kitchen (they call it the summer kitchen) where, standing at a table next to the window, looking at the apple trees bowing under the weight of their abundant branches, Elena recalls in her hoarse voice, always tainted with a rasping cough (she smokes excessively as she pours our glasses of whiskey, her long slightly curved back bent over the kitchen counter) the vanished Germany of her childhood, its wealth, its sumptuousness which are those of a fairy tale; but Elena says there's no cause for regret, it's just as well to have lost all that. If her incredibly rich family hadn't gone bankrupt, shortly before the Second World War, perhaps she would have been spared hunger, poverty, but she never would have understood that true life lies in simplicity, that's where one's faith in God is hidden, and that true love lies there as well, in such extreme deprivation.

"And we human beings are so pitiful we cannot live without loving, whether we love an animal or an object (Elena says, "A chair, we could love a chair when we're alone, that's how heavily solitude weighs..."), we can't live without love." Just back from an icy swim in the ocean, she rubs her rough hands together to warm herself; she has the hands of a sculptor, vigorous fingers with square tips. Elena's noble hands, I wonder whether the war didn't deform them a bit with the inferior tasks dictated by survival. Her hands are red, like her cheeks, whipped by the ocean breeze.

In the rays of the setting sun that emblaze the window towards which Elena turns occasionally to light a cigarette (she's never still for long, immobility is akin to self-indulgence for her), she busies herself with the cooking, she takes a loaf of bread out of the oven, waters a bouquet of daisies she picked that afternoon, along the roadside; her reddish blond hair has silver highlights at the temples, her broad forehead reveals her moral elevation, but there is no sign of pride. As we finish our glasses of whiskey, I don't know how to respond to Elena's affirmation "that men must be placed above women and a woman must respect and obey her husband." I tell her impolitely I don't believe a word of it, that such declarations are misguided. (In fact, under the influence of her daughter Helen who will soon be a flamboyant hippy and a rebellious flower child, Elena's ideas will change over the years.)

What disturbs me long after this conversation with Elena in the summer kitchen during my first visit to Cape Cod, what already exerts a divine attraction on me, is a story Elena tells in fits and starts and that I don't know how to interpret, it contains so many words from another place, veiled by her Germanic accent, but I can still hear that story I find so disturbing: a young seventeen year-old German, fearing the rise of Nazism in his country, drowns in a lake during an outing with some friends. Elena doesn't say who the boy is: a brother, a son, a friend? She dares not complain about any of her misfortunes and a painful mystery envelops her as she speaks to me, her face turned towards the window, her astonishing eyes staring at the horizon. What do we know of the people we meet? From what unknown hells have they emerged? I imagine the beauty of the blond boy, as Elena describes him to me. He's a young God, she says, I can see his classical features, the perfection of his face framed by the curls of his fine hair. Is it a dream? Did I hear right? Is this boy as beautiful as the other one who resembles him so closely (but who is alive and an American) whose picture I've seen on entering the dining room where the walls are covered with paintings and blue draperies? Elena tells me in a voice resigned to the impenetrable laws of destiny: "Believe me, with everything that was about to happen in Europe, that young man was lucky to die."

# Notebook 9

*obert is a young black writer* my age: he too has received a fellowship, and his first two books have garnered the praise of the New York critics. I meet him at the home of some professor friends in Cambridge, at the end of the decisive month of October 1963, shortly after my visit with Elena Wilson and the discovery of this group of writers and artists with whom I immediately felt a great affinity.

It's always with great difficulty that I return, after each visit with friends on Cape Cod, to the decrepit streets in my neighbourhood in Cambridge where destruction is spreading. For days I preserve the memory of the colourful houses in the dunes: they're blue, red and yellow like the houses of the Portuguese fishermen; the luminosity of the water nearby penetrates them, they seem brittle when the skies are overcast, as if the ocean could sweep them away. A painter who wears a beret and an apron stained with the shades of his water-colours lives isolated at the end of these sandy paths with their countless corridors leading to the sea; behind the screen door of his house, where the door stands open, a woman is writing, alone, her hair disheveled: it's Joan Colebrook, the indefatigable journalist and writer, always on the trail of the truth, investigating all the social systems, lies and injustices. It's noon:

her children with their blond hair (stridently blond in the sunlight) scramble down the dunes to the sea where they tickle the crabs with their bare feet.

Joan also writes about her faraway country of Australia, and such peacefulness, serenity only seems possible in this part of the world, amid these rolling hills and dunes. Robert, whose work has already met with a certain success, dreams of moving there, near Truro, where a white woman who loves him is waiting for him, he tells me as he drives me home to Broadway Street in his car (his father's, he says, for Robert is very proud to be a middle-class black man whose family lives on the outskirts of Boston, owners of flashy cars.)

No hope can survive misery, poverty, he tells me, noticing with distress the miserable neighbourhood where I live. He admits he's angry with the children of the ghetto who resort to violence. "It will bring nothing but death and suffering," he declares, with his usual moderation when he speaks of the young people who are daily victims of police brutality in the ghetto. "We're not in Alabama here, we're in New England... and the wind of freedom is blowing... If we stay calm, we'll get what we want, it's only through staying calm that my people can win the respect we deserve... the Black Panthers are going too far, it's not good for us... Martin Luther King is right... Non-violence is the only way... our only hope for salvation..."

The fight against segregation has exhausted Robert who now admits to having more personal preoccupations; he's going to be like his mentor, James Baldwin, the officially recognized writer of the Black Liberation movement, he'll go to live with the woman he loves in Paris, he'll be rich, free, happy, he says, and his tone of voice rises furiously as he runs his hand through his thick frizzy hair. He has the same rights as any other man. To prove it, he says, he's been warmly welcomed (he says, more softly, without prejudice) in the artists' and writers' colonies of Cape Cod, and as the critics emphasized, his masterful writing could be that of a Faulkner, a Flannery O'Connor... So, people should leave him free to live his life as he pleases.

In the years to come, I'll often see Robert walking with his companion, Jane, a painter, in the dunes of Truro; he'll remain moderate and indulgent towards our race, tender with the woman he lives with, but impenetrable behind his smile so quick to fade. Occasionally he'll remind us that James Baldwin, born in Harlem, managed to invest black writing with all its dignity, majesty; often, even at cocktail parties and celebrations, he'll remain mute at Jane's side.

One evening we have dinner together in Orleans, a fishing town illuminated by the pale light from the lighthouse blinking in the night; the restaurant also has a nautical decor, its nondescript wallpaper depicts a sunken ship tangled in its nets at the bottom of a coral reef. We drink wine and eat oysters, and Robert is cheered by the prospect of his next novel; suddenly he becomes sad when he mentions that this novel will be based on his childhood; I'm fascinated as he talks about Claude Brown (*Manchild in the Promised Land*), another promising young author of his generation praised by the critics, but it is Faulkner who inhabits him most of all, for in Faulkner Robert finds an assuaging, through the miracle of literature, of the great racial malaise.

Robert is suddenly speaking freely, and the hand he runs through his thick hair often pauses, as if he were stopping to think; he's convinced, he tells me, that it's a writer's imagination (more than life itself) that captures the reality of life. One need only compare the dreary county of Oxford with what Faulkner makes of it in his books: Benjy, Quentin, Christmas, Temple, the characters from *The Sound and the Fury*, from *Sanctuary*, and *Absalom, Absalom*, don't they come from the inner world that Faulkner describes in his books as the land of Yoknapatawpha? From this same hybrid country come the author's feelings, love as well as hate and especially total dissidence. We feel as if we're alone in this secluded place, Robert and I, talking about Faulkner to the sighing of wind in the dunes, in the glow of the lighthouse on the coast, and suddenly the conversation is interrupted by a malefic row of eyes looking daggers at us. Stunned, silent, we are prisoners of these eyes that would like to kill us.

We had been under the illusion, because we're in New England (and not in Alabama as Robert often says), that we'd gone beyond the scandalous line that still separates Blacks from Whites in the South, in public places. The people who are looking at us with such devastating hatred quickly make us realize how cruel the distance between Robert and me remains, how Robert's path will always be strewn with obstacles, for we are still at the point where Martin Luther King's dream remains only a dream.

# Notebook 10

*I*'m *staying in the cottage in the pines,* at Elena's house in Wellfleet, where everyone is invited to come to write in the silence of the country and everywhere you look, there are books. Here, as in the other house, the master's house, where Edmund writes in a mysterious closed room (where he sometimes invites particularly dear friends to share confidences), bookshelves line huge sections of the walls, and, on the bare wood floor, the only furnishings are those necessary to a writer: a table reminiscent of a school desk, a straightback chair, a lamp to light the blank page when night descends on the pine forest. This workroom is also the study of Reuel, Edmund's son from his marriage to the writer, Mary McCarthy. Reuel has his mother's elegant open-mindedness, her psychological subtlety in his relationships with others and, like his father, he is beginning to learn Hebrew. He's a brilliant linguist who appears to be able to read in all languages. I have not yet met this young man (who later will become a professor of Slavic languages at a Canadian university), but thanks to him, I enter the intimacy of this room where I contemplate a marvelous display of foreign literature: Flaubert and Gide, Goethe and Hesse, whom he reads in German, and Gogol and Dostoevsky, in Russian. All these books in Reuel's library intoxicate the imagination, exert such a hypnotic fascination that I can't manage to write in their presence. This simple cottage will host some extraordinary characters, Nabokov and, one day, Stalin's daughter shortly after her exile and the publication of a book on the atrocities of the Stalinist era. But, in this fall of 1963, we can still swim in the ocean; the ponds and lakes, soon to be frosty, are still sparkling in the clearings in the woods of Truro where a frightening couple lives, Gilberte and Anthony, and their son Christopher, whose face in my mind will always personify wounded innocence. If Anthony and Gilberte seem made to destroy each other, perhaps it's because they both suffer from the same inability to love; or perhaps this marriage between two individuals estranged by so many differences has become a source of alienation, of harassing weariness for both of them.

I've been reading for several hours in Reuel's library when Elena knocks on the door of the cottage, inviting me to take a walk with her, for it's a splendid autumn: in the woods of Truro where we walk, Anthony builds houses, with a view of the lake, that he rents to painters during the summer. Anthony is an architect and, when I see him that day, he is driving Christopher over a mountain of sand, in his truck, and he tells me how much he enjoys this good-natured child; "how can I feel discouraged and sad when I have such a cheerful child?" he asks. And it's Christopher's clear laughter we hear in the pond where he swims with me; standing on a raft a few feet from us, Anthony laughs and says that his son is lucky to have his future ahead of him, while he, Anthony, feels like an old man when he gets up in the morning, constantly depressed. I can't grasp the meaning of these comments coming from a man who lives in such an enchanted environment he had a hand in creating himself, in these woods, near these lakes and ponds where the Great Blue Herons land: his life seems heavenly to me, except for the fact that he and his wife Gilberte are always quarrelling, Gilberte, especially, often has devastatingly harsh things to say about her husband. That, too, is incomprehensible, since these two people could be united by their secret story: Anthony who, when angry, complains about the oppression of Judaism in his life, about the presence of a mother, a brilliant writer, who oppressed him without meaning to, is Jewish, and Gilberte, who was in the Resistance during the war, saved Jews, she says. They could have grave reasons for loving each other, yet I fear they hate each other. I listen to these words from Gilberte: "This man will never do anything with his life... He's weak...," and I feel a compassionate concern for Anthony. And he, so tall and strong, lowers his head as if his spine had been broken at birth. I feel very attracted to Anthony whose virility is seductive; despite his height and the strength apparent in all his gestures, he is vulnerable, almost fragile. And we get along well.

Gilberte has an angular face, fine features; her dark eyes are haunted by an anxiety always on the alert, because she is afraid of being destitute, as she was before: the memory of the concentration camps is still vivid, the spectre of hunger still hovers over the laden table. She bites her nails when she talks about this past of massacres, she smokes constantly, she also speaks of herself with pride, because Gilberte received honours for her heroism in France. But, she says bitterly, who knows that in these woods? Yet, when speaking of the superb houses Anthony builds, she says: "All this is mine, my property, my belongings..."

There was Reuel's room overflowing with books: there's Christopher's room where I come to write when Christopher is at boarding school in Vermont. From the window of this room, one can see a disturbing observation tower Gilberte had her husband build next to their house overlooking the lake. In the nightmares of a fitful sleep, one could hear, in this tower, the footsteps of a soldier surveying the horizon—that is what I think when I sleep in Christopher's bed, when I look at the cardboard towers he has built, in his games, these threatening towers lined up here beside me on the night table. Christopher tells his father he's going to be a sculptor, that he'll sculpt jewels and one can already sense his graceful skill in the execution of these towers, these fortresses. His room is also a padded shelter where the quarrelsome voices of his parents can't be heard, where he can draw during his school vacations, without being seen, devoting all his energy to the meticulous elaboration of these walls that protect him. After our swim in the pond, I watch him scramble, all wet, through an avalanche of sand, and his father's truck takes him away, humming through the woods. But that evening, in front of the fireplace, lying on the rug with a book, Christopher will once again hear the unhealthy whine of his parents' bickering, as they hurl insults at each other: "I hate you, why am I forced to live with you?"

It will go on like that season after season, for years: Christopher will soon go off to university, he'll leave to study sculpture in New York. One evening, when he's celebrating with friends the opening of an exhibition of his jewelry that promises to be a huge success, his mother phones him in New York; Christopher learns, brutally, that his father hanged himself a few feet from the doorstep of the new house he'd just finished near the lake. That is when Christopher's courageous face appears, its innocence and youth forever wounded. He returns home, he tries to console his mother who was hardened, scarred, by the concentration camps. He holds her in his arms. Again Gilberte says in her distress: "These are my belongings... my houses, my woods..." but she longs to escape from this pernicious domain. The observation tower still overlooks the house: from his bedroom window Christopher can see its shadow fall across the lake in the shape of a cross.

# Notebook 11

*I*n these turbulent years when the rapid, almost spontaneous, absorption of another culture seems to me so arduous, for the sixties are without a doubt one of the most tumultuous periods in American history, what requires the most courage and daring, of which I have so little, is my relationship with the unusual and marginal Americans I am beginning to meet during my visits to Cape Cod, at Elena's or Gilberte's house where I spend weekends, getting off the bus in Hyannis Port with my backpack, eager to feel the ocean breeze on my cheeks. Edmund Wilson, more than the others, with his inexorable erudition, his already venerable age (he is ten or fifteen years older than Elena) intimidates me when he says, emerging from his study to appear in the living room with the blue draperies where I'm reading with Elena (Elena makes a point of reading all the books her husband receives before giving them to him, so in my mind's eye I'll always see her with her head bent over a book), an amused smile floating on his round face: "If you came into my study, we could have a little chat." These words leave me totally disarmed: what are we going to talk about, how can I converse with this eminent critic who, once again, will emphasize the weaknesses of my style? ("It must be tighter," he'll say, "think of Rimbaud's poetry, he's very young, but it's very tight. Trim, trim, the flow needs to be more sustained, controlled.") Edmund and I don't hear the same music; he's barely aware, I tell myself, of the dazzling beginnings of the feminist revolution in North America. His generation of men is suspicious of women, in the aura of puritanism women are nothing but misled, perverse beings; this is how Baudelaire sees women too, essentially Christian, ever-guilty of leading men, chaste and virtuous, into a state of temptation.

Although I only sense them, I have a feeling of instinctive disgust for these ideas of Edmund's. But, today, Edmund shows none of this masculine vanity: wearing his kimono over a rather shabby brown suit, he comes over to me gently, extends his hand courteously to lead me into his study, a dimly-lit, silent room where, although his children tiptoe by silently and his wife withdraws as if at the threshold of a sanctuary, the family dog is allowed to enter (because he's so old, "the poor old boy"). Feeling inarticulate and ignorant, I watch Edmund settle into his Victorian chair, pressing to his chest a bottle of scotch (from which he pours me a glass full to the rim, although I'm in the most ascetic period of my life and drink very little), telling me he'll sleep better and have lovely dreams, tonight, once he's emptied the bottle, provided, he confides with a mischievous look, he can escape Elena's supervision. How can his wife forbid him a drink so good for his heart? When I see him so charming, relaxed, my fears seem absurd, today he won't talk about my style, nor about the young writers who write only one book in their life, especially women, and then die or get married. He immediately reassures me by talking about the books his wife is reading, "these days, theological philosophy, which I don't enjoy reading at all," he says firmly. "My wife also reads

Lautréamont, I don't like him... nor do I like the surrealists in general, aside from one or two painters, as for Gracq's work which you mention in your letter... I don't know it yet... You had time to write a play in Cambridge, you'll send it to me, won't you? If I don't have time, I'll have my wife read it first..." Edmund is leaving for Israel in a few days and his essay on Canadian literature is about to come out. He hopes nevertheless to celebrate Christmas with his grandchildren and show them the puppets he brought back from Japan.

Among the books by Québécois authors he's recently read, he expresses his admiration for *Pierre le magnifique* by Roger Lemelin (he says, "A lively, and likeable book, although I don't understand the hero."); *Poussière sur la ville* by André Langevin; he's begun reading *Chambres de bois* by Anne Hébert whose work intrigues him. He's devouring *Alexandre Chenevert, La petite poule d'eau, Rue Deschambault*, by Gabrielle Roy, touched by the humanism of these novels. He heartily recommends that I read Walter de la Mare, he says "he's an author with whom you'll find some similarities," and I hear him rattle off the titles of three short stories, *The Almond Tree, Out of the Deep, The Riddle*. With Edmund, whose life is woven with so many activities, trips and departures, I have to remember everything he tells me to read quickly, for these titles by Walter de la Mare, during our next conversation, will return like inquisitors, in Doctor Faustus' study. Edmund will ask: "Did you read the authors I recommended? What do you think of them? Do you remember the poem by Housman I love so much: 'Be still my soul, be still...' I read it at night..." Often these conversations will take place in the late afternoon, when the winter sun is setting on the dunes and the old dog lies snoring amid the old leatherbound books, when the scotch flows onto the ice in the glasses, and I'm overcome by the painful distress of suddenly feeling so far from home and so alone. When I open the door that separates me from the living room, I'll see Elena with Prince Paul and Nina Chavchavadze in their ghostly czarism, the dear friends Elena welcomes tenderly almost every day at six o'clock. Despite her age, her frail appearance, Nina works as a cleaning woman to survive; Elena says it's her only way of helping Paul who's writing a book on Czar Nicholas II and the destruction of the Romanov family, of which Nina is a descendant, with all its pomp and wealth, she who works as a humble servant in American households here on the Atlantic coast. "That is secular sainthood," says Elena, "that's what some people must endure. Such a road of sorrow, and pain..." We are all equal in this living room with the blue draperies where I, as insecure as I am, feel less frightened of others even if their history is longer, or even from another age in some cases. The light is still on in Edmund's study, he'll spend the night writing, he'll hear the words from Housman's poem, as he listens to the erratic beating of his sick heart, pressing the bottle of scotch to his breast, in his solitude he'll hear: "Be still my soul, be still..."

# Notebook 12

*It's a grey day* in November 1963, I've been writing since morning, but struggling with the words, without really understanding the meaning of what I'm doing, as often happens at the beginning of a story, of a novel where a multitude of ideas, of images overlap, dispersed in a haze; what worries me most on this grey day is the feverish mood rippling through the streets of Cambridge, especially on Broadway Street where crowds of rowdy young people gather in front of the store windows, pushing and shoving but never taking their eyes off the blue screen broadcasting President Kennedy's arrival in Dallas. I'm alone in my room and I'm writing, still shaken by the stomping of the crowds in the streets; what does the day have in store for us? Is the Earth going to explode? An incomprehensible furor seems to be rumbling outside and the fluidity of words, of sentences eludes me like a face obscured by pain. In an awkward gesture, I knock everything off my work table, a pencil, then a book slips from from my hands, the medallion I'm wearing around my neck breaks, falls to my feet with a dull thud. On my way home from the Harvard library by bike, I heard the deadly news on the radio, I read it on the lips of the black boys I passed in the street and I too am submerged by the wave of

*Nov. 1963*

terror which in times of disaster forces the soul to contemplate its own nothingness.

What will become of us all? What world of ultimate calamities are we living in? In every household in North America, everyone is listening, stunned, to the startling message on their radios, televisions, transmitting in the November fog the sinister news, and that day everyone's heart shudders with a sense of the end of the world.

And yet, this shudder will be felt several times again, during these years of bloodthirsty madness, and gradually perhaps, we'll become indifferent to the uneasiness, the powerful confusion it awakens in us.

I can't stay in this room another minute, I have to be with other people, lose myself in the griefstricken crowd. I throw on my coat—a beige duffle coat with a hood, bought at the Harvard Co-op, in which I feel impersonal, everyone around me is dressed the same way—groups of young people have gathered in a state of shock in front of the television screens in the store windows many of which have been shattered; police cars are patrolling all around us in the funereal haze of this day where smoke and blood seem to rise from the earth and we rush over to each other, regardless of language or race, asking incredulously: "Is it true? Is it true? Did we hear right?" And we learn from one another that, yes, it is true. In schools and colleges, classes are interrupted to announce to the students, yes, that's really what happened, there's nothing we can do about it, it's a terrible tragedy. On the Harvard campus, students cry in each other's arms, people are crying everywhere, in schoolyards, here in the streets of Cambridge, of

Boston, where Blacks and Whites march together, united by the same sudden brutal loss; everyone is reeling from the shock, crumpled faces, slumped bodies, sob with pain. It's a day when the God people pray to in churches and temples, the vehement God of the Bible, has struck mankind, sparing none.

Jack, who's been wandering as he does every afternoon along the banks of the Charles River where, between two courses, he can take his Acid without being seen, tells me, looking gaunt, shivering from the cold in his raincoat, his hair pulled back in a ponytail that covers his neck with dirty curls—recently Jack has been neglecting his appearance and the money his parents send from Ohio is spent entirely on drugs, his appearance is often that of a derelict—Jack tells me, his whole body trembling with emotion: "President Kennedy has been assassinated. My youth is over... President Kennedy was assassinated today and, in Dallas, it was sunny... I heard the sound of the three shots that killed him and I died too..." Yet I remember that Jack did not approve of President Kennedy's politics, that he considered him responsible for the escalating war in Vietnam, but the same Jack who condemned the blindness of a man in power suddenly understands the man who was only John F. Kennedy to his family, an individual both charismatic and familiar, whose photograph can be seen in American homes everywhere; I also find it in Elena's house, in her summer kitchen, this familiar vigilance of a young president universally loved. Elena often looks with admiration, deference, at this picture in the middle of a wall where the president smiles his wholesome, loyal smile, as if he were there in the family's midst, like a friend, a brother, a man of good faith who, despite his mistakes, is seeking peaceful coexistence among nations; but behind the tense-jawed smile of the young hero, one cannot guess the designs of this ambitious man, stoic in his physical suffering.

During this implacable decade of the sixties, the American people will often march through the streets spilling tears that still flow thirty years later when the memory of the deceased president is honoured on television, in the press. And we also remember, with the same anger, Martin Luther King's assassination—and we remember that by a perverse twist of fate, it was gentle Robert Kennedy, so close to the Blacks, who announced in Washington the news of the murder that had just been committed, merciless fate, for shortly after that, Robert, the one who had preserved the integrity of his ideals, was also shot to death. On this grey day in November 1963, on the Harvard University campus young people are crying: "My God, how can we go on living in this violent country? How can we survive so many atrocities?" We walk through the streets, reeling, ashamed of this society where so many other murders will soon take place, where murderers even kill each other—as we'll see live on television with the death of Lee Harvey Oswald. In these times of mourning and massacres, the images of the women, the widow of a president, of a preacher, behind their black veils, will haunt our memories; in these women, each of us will recognize some of our own grief. We will share the burden of their loss. For young people they will embody motherhood, which gave birth to life, not death, bewailing the violence mankind has begotten.

# Notebook 13

*ho are these women?* Mary Meigs, Barbara Deming. During my brief visits to Wellfleet at Elena's, and at Gilberte and Anthony's house near the lake in Truro, I often hear people mention their names, the exceptional nature of the friendship they've shared for years, and the strength of character of these two women so very different from one another. In this summer of 1963, as they will every summer, they've fled the noisy dunes of Cape Cod invaded by tourists, to live in the isolation of an old farmhouse that doesn't even have electricity; but like other artists from New York—the painters Anne and Henry Poor, and Bill Cummings, who founded the Skowhegan School of Painting and Sculpture where I'll hear the music of John Cage for the first time, where I'll even see Cage himself spontaneously inventing his music in the barn where young painters gather every evening, eager for avant-garde experiments in music and art—like all of these artists, Barbara and Mary are attracted by the silence of a pastoral life in the woods and the fields of these isolated regions, still undiscovered, where abandoned farms, dilapidated cabins are transformed into painting, writing or sculpture studios, where oil lamps glow through misty windowpanes at night, because it rains a lot in Maine and at dusk the fields begin to glisten beneath the warm raindrops and the veil of distilled mist that slowly rises.

In Wellfleet, when I see Mary's and Barbara's houses, nestled in the hills above a little country road called Pamet Point Road, along which you can ride your bike down to the bay, I imagine the intellectual exhilaration of these two women surrounded by their work, their dogs and their cats, in these hills where the wild roses bloom; I don't think I can imagine anything more beautiful, more noble, than this kind of freedom where, by mutual consent, each woman, with all her fierce individualism, is passionately, fervently absorbed in the expression of her creativity. I know that Mary is a painter and Barbara, a writer. I also know that they live without any concessions to the society they were born into, a liberal society perhaps—that of the American upper or middle class, the society in which Henry James was raised—but one that still harbours, despite its liberalism, archaic attitudes towards women. People are not ashamed to say—as they do of black people—that women are third-class citizens. Barbara and Mary's way of thinking, of being, as independent women, proving that they can live without men, is more than progressive—it is seen as a shocking provocation. And this delights me: at last in the too conventional world of this wealthy community of artists on Cape Cod, I hear some individual, dissident voices that refuse to be silenced.

At the time, it doesn't occur to me that the freedom Mary and Barbara have acquired is, for a woman, a difficult right to defend. As the years go by, I'll realize just how long-term this struggle is. Yet I could have simply recalled my conversation with Edmund about Virginia Woolf, when we were sitting together on the park bench and I noticed one of his shoelaces trailing on the grass at our feet; that day, Edmund told me: "I'll introduce you to two extraordinary women, Mary and Barbara. You'll see that Virginia Woolf's world is not so far removed from ours. But I share Ernest Hemingway's thoughts on this subject: I think the only valid relationships are relationships between men and women. These are the only supreme relationships. The rest," he said speaking of Gertrude Stein, "love between people of the same sex, isn't it like a glove made for the left hand worn on the right? Nevertheless, as my wife said, Barbara, who is one of the most radical activist poets in this country—which makes us all worry about Mary because Barbara is often arrested—as my wife, whose judgement is often skewed by her faith but this time she's right, would say, Barbara is a saint, and I must say that personally I care little about people's private lives, but of course in our community, although accustomed to a certain open-mindedness, we're a bit surprised to see women living without men...Two women as attractive as they both are and they're not even fifty. We find it intriguing. I hope they're happy like this. But I doubt it... a woman can only find fulfillment with a man and her children."

Gilberte's comments will be very similar: "They remind me of two inseparable friends I knew in the concentration camps, inseparable even at the time of their death... I thought, the poor women, they're going to be executed without ever knowing what it's like to be loved by a man... and I often think of those two young women when I see Mary and Barbara."

During a lunch in Cambridge with Mary, not long after our Virginia Woolf conversation, Edmund is so touching with Mary, so solicitously gentle, that I see in him an endearing man, incredibly charming with women. I even see in him a man who can change, whom the constant company of a woman like Elena has already considerably refined. Mary is so shy I hardly dare look at her that day. Edmund is there, reassuring; we speak in French, about the exhibition of self-portraits by Van Gogh we're going to see at the Fogg Museum.

As we stand in front of one of those paintings by Van Gogh, Mary tells me about her own painting, and about a series of self-portraits she is constantly reworking in her studio; although she's never quite satisfied with them, each one of these drawings, these paintings, is an unfinished revelation of herself she must pursue. Such intransigence touches me, the ochre and gold hues of Van Gogh's paintings captivate my gaze as Mary talks about her work, about her solitary battle in her studio in the red house on the hill. She rises very early, she says, is learning Spanish, beginning to read the poets Gabriela Mistral and Rosalia Castro, paints all day, practices piano and flute in the evening, she is a flutist with the Provincetown Symphony Orchestra. I sense in her a vast mind that knows no borders. The ochre and gold hues of Van Gogh's paintings, those obsessive colours swirling like the demented painter's suns, surround us, surround Mary's face in the dim light, until I can see only a fringe of bangs over a broad forehead.

# Notebook 14

*It's an icy, damp winter* in Cambridge, with very little snow, but rain glazes the streets where we still ride our bicycles. I spend long hours writing in my room, or, when the cold makes it impossible, I go to the Harvard library where students weigh the difficulty of their assignments, holding their heads in their hands, surrounded by their reference books.

Mary calls me regularly, concerned about my comfort in this basement heated by a single defective radiator that gives off little heat. She informs me sadly that Barbara has been sent to jail in Birmingham, arrested with her friends during a massive demonstration against racism in the South of the United States.

This is the winter of 1963, when the voice of a racist dictator like Wallace can be heard on television daily. Today it seems inconceivable that such a pernicious person proclaiming his rejection of racial integration could not only be heard, but even encouraged, acclaimed by the segregationist mood of the era. Since 1961, Barbara has participated in several peace marches, she was in fact one of the first white activists to speak out against racism. In 1963, black schools and churches are being bombed in Birmingham, children are being killed, black students murdered in the streets. The youths from the ghetto in my neighbourhood watch the blue screen in store windows transmit the cruel eloquence of George Wallace, inciting his followers to exterminate the black race. Beneath the hypocrisy of his speeches in which the name of God is often pronounced, there is a true hatred of Blacks and a virulent incitement to violence.

How can one write about anything except one's feeling of injustice when living in an atmosphere charged with rumours of war, brutality and such overtly expressed racism? Nevertheless, I try to write every day, and this act seems to be the only decent and useful act I can perform during these months of apprehension, when students on all American campuses are demonstrating their concern about the war in Vietnam.

The portraits I sketch in my notebooks are drawn from live models during my visits to Cape Cod; they're no more than hasty sketches, but I want to preserve the intensity of these unexpected moments in this new country where so many faces suddenly reveal some of their more subtle and secret traits, as I draw closer and try to capture a likeness. There is Elena's beauty and the glow of her candid faith when she speaks of the sainthood she respects in the most humble of people, the saintly strength which I call, during our discussions in her summer kitchen in Wellfleet, a legitimate struggle to survive with dignity all the troubles, the losses and upheavals we must face during a lifetime on earth—but especially her beauty, beaming like a golden halo over every word she speaks, each one stamped by her slightly harsh accent, like a song where emotion is contained and abandon sternly repressed.

Yet I can't help but rebel when I see this woman whose knowledge is so vast and diverse fall modestly silent in the presence of her husband whose intellectual stature she reveres, and whom she admires quite simply because he's a man. I feel the same rebellion when I overhear Gilberte speaking harshly to her husband; I consider Anthony a misunderstood man whose pride is constantly scorned, trampled; there is such mistrust in his eyes, such embarrassment lurks in his smokey gaze flecked with gold, like that of felines, when he hears what Gilberte thinks of him. These women have all offended him, his mother, his sisters with their insolence, and now Gilberte, this woman he brought back from France and who never stops taunting him with tales of her heroism during the war while she languishes in her domain, near the lake, wandering from one house to another in her querulous boredom, for Gilberte complains all day about being poor, while Anthony wears himself out, building houses with his own hands, hoping to make her rich.

There's Robert, the black writer who walks through the dunes of Truro with Jane on his arm; in the village people whisper that this woman twenty years older than Robert is dying of cancer, they lower their voices during the cocktail parties in the grey-shingled houses lit by a fire on the hearth and say, "how awful for them, they love each other so much." The mysterious disease eating away at this beautiful, sensual woman on Robert's arm, the woman he never lets out of his sight, whom he accompanies once a week to the hospital in Hyannis Port, is masked by Jane's unshakable determination to live.

Closer to home, here in Cambridge, my bicycle brushes Jack's dilapidated bicycle as we skid through the icy streets. Since President Kennedy's death, Jack rarely attends his classes at the university, he's often alone, freezing to death in his clothes, floundering along the sidewalks on his bicycle, still wearing the same threadbare raincoat he wore all summer. "My parents don't want to send me any more money," he says "I haven't eaten for three days, it doesn't matter, I'm not hungry." Sweat streams down Jack's forehead, he absolutely has to find some LSD today, or he'll throw himself into the Charles River. His life is a nightmare, he says, nobody wants to help him, even the drug rehabilitation centres refuse to deal with him now, because he keeps going back to his habits, he repeats in an incoherent monologue that he'd like to found a family, have a wife and children.

Jack is one of the faces that make me sad. I don't know whether I should avoid him or invite him to have coffee with me. I feel as if he isn't responsible for his careless existence: like so many others, he is the victim of a euphoria whose dangers were discovered belatedly. Consuming LSD is now illegal.

A friend from Québec, about to embark upon a trip around the world, comes to camp out in my apartment shortly before Christmas, and as he sets his backpack down on a chair, I'm overwhelmed by an almost urgent desire to leave with him; my life in this cold room, in this country whose politics I cannot abide, whose warmongering aberrations are about to engulf us all, this can't be the life I'd choose for myself.

In the throes of these confusing thoughts, in the company of a friend I know so well, perhaps too well, there's a phone call from Mary who wants to share her joy at having done a painting, "another self-portrait in colours that sing," she says, "and I don't often see colours sing, so it's a good day after all. Tomorrow I'll rework the facial expression, I find it too sulky, I don't like the curve of the mouth." Mary's voice, speaking slowly, unsure of herself, with a tinge of melancholy, suddenly convinces me without hesitation to stay here where, without my knowing how or why, a gruff angel named Edmund guided me, here in the folds of American life, with its shadows and its glimmers of hope and light, confined to my work cell in Cambridge.

# Notebook 15

*Often during these winter walks* by the sea with Elena who swims late in the season, we speak of the cultural bond we both feel with Europe. The aristocratic Europe Elena knew before World War II is not the Europe I knew during the year I spent in France, at age twenty, along with other recipients of Canada Council grants: actors, painters, students at the Sorbonne beginning their doctoral studies. But Elena loves France and French literature, and is curious to know how one is treated as a writer from abroad, just starting out, in Paris. Was that the day she expressed her misgivings about Simone Weil's ideas? "She died too young," says Elena, while for me, Simone Weil's youth, the candour of her spiritual emancipation, her quest for God fraught with doubt, and an instinctive mistrust of the autocracy of Churches, the rigidity of their principles, these are the strengths of a life still experienced as an offering, or hesitating between the celebration of the joy of living and the painful awareness soon to be inflicted by the war. I evoke for Elena, although afraid I'll shock her with the amoral tendencies often associated with the freedom of young people in the sixties in the eyes of a woman who still believes in sin, my life with my friends in the room we shared in a Paris hotel, Hotel L'Aiglon, in Montparnasse, where thanks to our miraculously tolerant hotel-keepers, and also because the French are so fond of Canadians, we all find accommodation for the modest sum of sixty dollars a month. There's the boys' room and the girls' room which includes a kitchen and bathroom. And we wander from one room to the other with our bottles of wine, our sandwiches, and we share the same bidet, this object we find so incongruous, for washing the clothes usually thrown into a weekly heap on the tile floor. We have trouble making ends meet, our resources are limited, but Claire-France oversees the budget of our household where the francs in the common cup are counted daily for the purchase of food. There are many days without meat, always met with grouchy protests from Marc, Jean, André, François, but green beans and fish are also excellent for these boys whose growing period is not yet over, although to me they all seem so strong and muscular, with the exception of Marc, Claire's fiancé, who has, she says, the lanky looks of the hero in Alain-Fournier's novel, *Le Grand Meaulnes*. Claire-France is part of the wave of prolific young women writers; she has attracted considerable attention with her first novel, *Les enfants qui s'aiment*, as has Françoise Sagan at the same time in Paris with her marvelous and lucid *Bonjour tristesse*, as has another young girl, Minou Douet, whose voice delights everyone with nostalgic poems of an otherworldliness that could be the timeless paradise of Rimbaud's *Illuminations*. Suddenly people are listening to the voices of these women, these young girls, although publishers don't understand their fragility, the delicate sensitivity that brings a welcome respite from the weary writing of men, warriors, fighters. But these prodigal children of another era, released from the depths of the female soul, this exquisite literature quite incompatible with the other, heavier fare, finally arouses the financial interest of publishers who suddenly want to publish us, although our books are virtually untamed expressions of adolescence and its wild impulses. We are a world apart. Claire's precociousness in the civilized world of Paris publishers sees us through a cocktail party, a gathering hosted by an important publisher and members of his family in their ancestral garden; she tells me how to behave, lends me a silk dress in a floral print, I feel despicable in it and I can hear it rustle on my back, but we must emerge from this test victorious. Claire is intransigent with me, and as painful as I find the depth of my ignorance at the time, my inability to cope with any literary scene whatsoever, a pale light leads me back to that garden, to the luncheon with the Flammarion family: it's the memory of a blond woman braiding a bouquet of flowers with her son in short pants who welcomes us with a nod of the head when she notices us on the pathway, Claire and me. Claire who is intrepid, strides joyfully down the garden paths with her brown curls bouncing around her confident face. But while Claire satisfied her publishers' expectations by selling thousands of copies of her books, a very different experience awaits me; my first novel will be awarded a medal by the Académie française, the prize for a first novel, I believe, but the sales will be so scant Mr. Dickerman, our fiction editor, will feel sorry for me. Nevertheless, I'll receive a cheque for almost three hundred francs, enough to hitchhike around Europe with Louise, an actor friend, sleeping in farmhouses in the Jura, wending our way to Venice; in another attempt to console me, the kind fiction editor will take me in his old Volkswagen with its collapsing seats and whining engine, on a pilgrimage to Chartres, and, on the following Sunday, although these Sundays seem so long and boringly precious, to the cathedral in Reims. "Here, my dear child," he tells me, "you have true culture."

But I've read a great deal of Gide, and gradually his works and those of Proust will become frequent subjects of conversation between my friend and me. When I'm shunted aside one Sunday in favour of a visit with a godson studying philosophy in a provincial boarding school, I suddenly miss my friend who spoke so subtly of Gide on the otherwise bland Parisian Sundays where my friends and I idle away our time, penniless, unable even to go to the cinema; the boys go to visit their mistresses, they boast of their feats in the evening as we sit down to our plates of overcooked, gelatinous fish, and tasteless green beans. Claire and I type away on the white typewriter we share, but Sundays take us off guard, each left to her thoughts over a cold cup of coffee.

It's undoubtedly because I find Minou Drouet's writing so dazzling (although it might be the brilliance of a fleeting inspiration, as if this young girl wanted to make us hear the sound of celestial bells, then disappear as quickly as she came), that I dare write to Professor Pasteur-Valléry-Radot, primarily to congratulate him for having understood the clarity of this childlike voice that sometimes has the grave resonance of the voice of a prophet. For several years we'll write to each other; in 1960, we'll meet several times, and in the company of these people from other eras, other cultures, my European education will begin.

It's the winter of 1963, New Year's Eve is not far away, this is Elena's last swim in the already frigid waves of the ocean. Back on the beach, she wraps herself in a rough wool sweater, the same intense blue as her eyes, like the draperies in her house, the insistently dense and variable blue of the ocean is all around her; we walk along the beach strewn with driftwood, the gulls dive into the waves, soar above our heads. Elena falls silent, she must get back to the house quickly: Edmund is waiting for her with the Saturday papers, it's time to make sweet apple jam, to stack the wood for the winter, to write to Helen in her Swiss boarding school, to read *La source grecque*, and once again, I'll learn nothing about Elena's Europe of which she only says: "There was a time when our country was so beautiful..." and then silence descends upon the waves as the sun sets on this shore of the Atlantic.

# Notebook 16

*They are elderly painters*, engravers, sculptors, who have retired to the Cape where they live year round, in the wooded hills of Truro, in the wintry mists of Provincetown, where they watch from their grey-shingled houses, from the gabled windows of their studios, the steamships arrive on a sea caught in the diaphanous light of fog at twilight, like a painting by Turner where you can feel the passing storm, the imminent gale.

They fled the persecution of the Jews in Europe, and here in this land of their ultimate refuge, America, they were once again persecuted for their ideology, their dissidence, when they chose to become Communists, socialists. I meet Eugene and Ella, the painter Karl Knaths, through Mary who often visits them and buys their work; in the sixties, they are pacifists and they believe that their art should bear witness to their indignation against the Vietnam War which has plunged university campuses across the country, from Harvard to Berkeley, into a state of anxiety and mourning.

Their art, which they create in silence, scurrying around their studios in their blue painters' smocks, evolves as they do, quietly, with a gentle constancy, a tranquil impermeability to the changing times. Monastic and introspective, they sculpt statuettes in their gardens, in a flight of fancy, they paint mermaids on the walls of their houses. In the summer, the table in the middle of the garden near the fountain where swallows come to drink and bathe is often set with glasses of cherry drinks glistening in the sun, with plates of fruit and cheese for the visiting son who lived in Russia while writing an essay on Dostoevsky. Grandchildren also come to visit Eugene and Ella Jackson who contemplate them briefly, their paintbrushes poised in mid-air, in a moment of distracted pleasure, for their thoughts are elsewhere, stalking the subtle changes in the sky that have to be painted quickly, in the splash of turquoise-blue gouache soon to invade the still white canvas waiting on the easel.

For the painter Karl Knaths, who is an elderly man with clear grey eyes under bushy white eyebrows, the symbol of the dove of peace appears often, like Picasso's dove; painters Wally Putnam and Leonid who spend long hours sketching on the beach paint the same bird in silhouette, a tiny bird, a solitary creature in the immensity of a windswept landscape, whose feet drag along the sand, whose wings cannot fly.

In the fog that grows thicker around the village of Provincetown as the long winter and the cold set in, the painters are nowhere to be seen, the wind off the water rattles the closed shutters, no one lives here in the winter, except for these few individuals hidden away with their gouache and oil paints who only come out, it would seem, to buy art supplies at the Studio Shop where suddenly, in the middle of the sketchbooks, the still-intact canvasses, the tubes with a texture or a mysterious radiance on paper which they've yet to discover, they stand beaming under their sailor's caps, huddled together around a woodstove, their souls aglow again. They casually exchange a few words about their choice of materials, for solitude weighs on each of them and who knows whether the elderly painter Karl will still be with them next winter? Each one resumes his pilgrimage through the fog to his house where the smell of fresh paint on the latest canvas lures him back to his easel and brushes.

Ella and Eugene, in their adjoining studios in the hills, offer criticism of each other's work. Eugene with his snowy white hair, his milky and rosy complexion, listens, his head cocked over his wife's shoulder, to the advice she proffers with unshakable love: why did Eugene study block printing so late, he who is so talented, asks Ella, and what is the shape in this drawing, why can't we tell whether it's an animal or a human being? Eugene, who discovered his passion for engraving at the age of eighty—before that he was a grammarian, on the table near the fireplace in the living room lie the text books he wrote: German grammar, Russian grammar, Greek grammar, these books he finds boring in his old age, he says, and they were written so long ago, they smell musty—Eugene defines the shape on his wood block, this thing that is neither animal nor human, as himself, beset by the vicissitudes of aging, and Ella, who is sturdy, buxom, at the side of her frail, snowy-haired husband to whom she is dearest friend and enormous love, grumbles that her husband exaggerates, that nothing is as sinister as what he sees in the black phantoms of his prints.

But Eugene proves to be right, he and Karl will be the first to disappear into those wintry mists from which they will never return. And alone for many years in her garden in the summer,

Ella will greet us with her vodka and cherry drinks, the table set beneath the trees. Amid the paintings, the statuettes, the mermaids on the walls of the house, she'll greet Mary and me, spreading her arms before the paintings where we'll recognize the same table in the garden and the effervescent colours of jonquils in their china vases.

An accident, while taking a walk with Mary, in the woods along Pamet Point Road, the road that leads from Truro bay to Provincetown, silent in the winter fog, an apparently banal incident (a branch snapped back and hit my eye) will seem to change my life, to reshape it, since it will virtually deprive me for a while of the use of my left eye. This accident that will force me to rest, to abruptly suspend work on my novel, will lead me to discover in drawing, painting, the play of shapes and colours, a lasting exploration of this art form that can bring such enchantment, so many delightful surprises.

Adrift in this long winter's night where I can hardly use my eyes, where I am as disoriented in Cambridge as on Cape Cod, I perceive the extreme vulnerability of the body so intimately linked to what we never truly appreciate as long as we possess it: sight. The red sign over the door of the Studio Shop in Provincetown, cloaked in the fog from the sea, beckons to me, guides me, as if it were a sign of my cure, and of my desire to see. I continue on toward the studios where these elderly painters with failing, soon to be extinguished eyesight, stooped over their drawings, their canvasses, teach me that a blaze of colours glows there, at their fingertips, and there lies the return of light.

Through this wound in my left eye also penetrates the knowledge of pain, and the patience it requires, with oneself. At times it seems as if everything enters through this sharp breach: the peril of this struggling country where I have ventured, the joy of opening my eyes to the sunlight one morning, the concern and pain of knowing that Barbara is fasting in a horrible Birmingham jail, along with a group of militant companions including Yvonne Klein, and the impotence of realizing that, although I don't yet know Barbara, I cannot help her in this hour of need.

# Notebook 17

*It's snowing in Cambridge*, the bicycles have been stored in the hallways of the apartment building where, even under lock and chain, they'll be stolen when someone distractedly leaves a door wide open onto the back yard, inviting hoodlums to come search the mailboxes for pension cheques destined for retired tenants.

It's in this winter of 1963 that I begin to write *A Season in the Life of Emmanuel*: these few months of writing will be very difficult, everything seems to resist me, nothing I write seems worthwhile, the money from the fellowship has been spent; writing the story of Jean-le Maigre leaves me weak, I want him to be graceful, not seeming to bear alone like so many poets—I think of Kafka, Rilke—the debt of all humanity, its evils, its cruelty; I want him to be proud, ardent, spirited and cheerful, but the weight of the task overwhelms me; I write a page and I have to lie down, everything seems compromised by my health concerns.

Reading a biography of Keats, I understand why poets die at twenty—their experience goes back to times that precede the years of their life, they are vested with the memory of distant impressions, and the pressure to describe these impressions, these recollections of a universal memory, this pressure is so great it upsets the stability of body and soul. Suddenly one feels completely defeated, broken. Perhaps this explains Virginia Woolf's madness when she was writing *The Voyage Out* and *To the Lighthouse*, Kafka's tuberculosis while writing *The Trial, The Penal Colony*; that which goes beyond personal memory also comes from infernal regions often unknown to us.

I don't know where Jean-le Maigre and his family come from, but as I struggle over this novel, I know that they exist somewhere. That I must talk about them to soften the blow of their destiny. "These seven year-old poets," as Rimbaud said, have been abandoned around the world, stranded in poverty-stricken countrysides from which they cannot escape, victims of ignorance and religious oppression. They have been raped and murdered and continue to die every day. The factories in the cities have stunted them as well, I've seen their faces, the despondency visible in their eyes, they will not survive their enslavement. Here in my ghetto in Cambridge, I see Jean-le Maigres shining the shoes of white men, who have nothing but contempt for these children—if they were born poets, their works will never be written. They will be drug addicts, they'll go to prison, perhaps they will be child criminals.

In contrast to my life while writing this novel, a life lacking all luxury, the intellectual circles I frequent that have nurtured and supported me since I met Edmund, Elena and Mary, this elite lives well, though their comfort is simple, without abundance, and they want to share this comfort with me when I flounder in doubt, despair. When I finally complete the novel, once Mary and Edmund have read it, I'll have more self-confidence and suddenly I'll feel cured, amazed by the sudden release.

During this winter of doubt, reading sometimes brightens my life. The delight of reading *The Company She Keeps* by Mary McCarthy, the joy of listening to Mary read to me in Spanish, Rosalia Castro, Gabriela Mistral. I marvel that these works were written by women, beneath the disguise of poetry or fiction, I admire the incredible bravery of these authors who speak about themselves with such frankness.

I am touched by such totally concrete writing, as finely executed as a musical score. The courage in Mary McCarthy's writing will guide her personal life too, and her political commitment when she goes to Vietnam, when she denounces the bombing of Hanoi, along with the poet Robert Lowell. She will encourage young writers and, many years later, in the company of her charming husband, James, in their apartment in Paris on rue de Rennes, she'll introduce me to the woman who wrote *L'opponax*, Monique Wittig, one of the most dazzling feminist writers of her generation.

But in this winter of 1963 when I'm engaged in a constant battle with myself as I write, I'm unapproachable, unsociable. I'll leave Cambridge for a while, to lock myself up in Mary's house in Wellfleet, a few feet from her studio in the woods, in a part of the house that once served as an ironing room. In this room that separates me from the world, this room I'll seldom leave until winter's end, I'll silently descend into the lives of Jean-le Maigre and his brothers, and although my health is no better, I'll feel less alone in my struggle with all these writers close by, these artists for whom writing, music, painting is the sacred goal of their lives.

Even when Jean-le Maigre's death has been consummated, the battle is not over. Several publishers in Québec will reject the manuscript. Perhaps they are embarrassed by the evocation of a society so oppressive and oppressed, or is the reminder of this dark period in Québec's history simply too painful to bear? Jean-le Maigre's poetry, his insolent way of playing with words escapes them. But then there is Jacques Hébert, there is someone who listens, who knows how to draw a writer and a work out of the shadows. And Québec will soon discover the prodigious writers he was the first to recognize: Michel Tremblay, Victor-Lévy Beaulieu, Nicole Brossard, Michèle Mailhot and many others. Yet every one of my books, in the early phases of their creation, will bring the same mental anguish, and the same physical torment.

One is never satisfied with oneself, the work is inhuman and one suddenly feels so unsure of one's strength, so disarmingly fragile. One has to grapple with the uncertainty, the fear of getting lost in the complex paths of the imaginary which are nonetheless paved with true and grave realities. Perhaps it's the torment of this uncertainty that caused the brutal death of a brilliantly talented man like Hubert Aquin. Essentially, giving birth to a life is a never-ending task. And in giving a bit of life to that which is not yet alive, one dies a bit oneself.

# Notebook 18

*riting* sometimes attracts strange coincidences. Here in Key West, many years later, while I attempt to sketch the individuals I knew during those days in Wellfleet, Edmund, Elena, Gilberte, Anthony and several others, I dream of them at night as if they were still alive.

In one of these dreams Elena says to me: "What is a Christian death?", speaking to me as naturally as if we were back in the sun-filled summer kitchen, in her white house with the blue curtains, her gaze as sparkling and lively as it was then; she is with some young girls who seem to be her students or disciples, for in the brief eternity of my dream, I see her pursuing her spiritual quest, transmitting it to young people.

My meeting with Edmund takes place in a train station where he is waiting for a departing train. He is dressed in a beige linen suit and wearing a hat. When he sees me, there is the usual trace of irony in his smile; tipping his hat, he asks politely: "Which train will take me there?" The distance separating us seems almost palpable, as if these presences in my dreams became visibly incarnate, flesh and blood, despite the transparency of their conversation.

My days are not, however, spent with them. I'm totally obsessed by the novel I'm writing, so much so I must be a burden to anyone kind enough to spend time with me in such a state of concentration and inner tension; even when I venture out at midday, my notebook comes with me so I can trace every move of my characters, Carlos and his black brothers on the outskirts of Bahama Village.

Sometimes these days are most unsatisfactory and become a source of tension, of psychological discomfort. When the weight of this self-imposed rigour makes your heart feel as if it's about to explode in your chest, it's best to leave the novel, the poem or the text to its own devices, and renew your strength for the freshness of another day, seeking distraction elsewhere.

Friends have a way of appearing miraculously at that point. Jacinthe, who's spent the day making jewelry in the blazing sun of Duval Street, in the artists' square, invites me go out with her that night. The evening is an improvisation, like an aimless stroll; what we both want most that night is to forget our work and the drudgery it entails, whether it be in the glaring sun with the all too often vulgar tourists or alone in the little room on the top floor under the ceiling fan that purrs overhead while I write, facing daily the doubts and distress that entails. We raise our glasses to toast Matsu on the terrace of a restaurant that was once the Café Exile where he used to play with his group of jazz musicians.

We recall the difficult period when Matsu was so persevering, back in the days when Jacinthe and the young Japanese musician were in love, "and in those days," says Jacinthe, "Matsu was sleeping in a closet, but we were happy anyway."

This is the week of the Literary Seminar in Key West, and this year it's dedicated to Elizabeth Bishop and her work. Since I work every morning, I've been unable to attend the talks, but in fact these literary gatherings make me very uncomfortable. I can imagine how eloquently and perceptively my friends James Merrill, John Malcolm Brinnin and all the other invited speakers must have honoured the memory of this great poet and her spare, unadorned verse, but there is always too much socializing involved in these events.

It's much more pleasant to see John and Jimmy in the secluded garden at David's house on Elizabeth Street, or elsewhere in town, in the intimacy of a real get-together. That particular evening, Jacinthe suggests we go to feed the cat we call Bob Tail, our orphan of the day at the Hemingway House, where in fact all cats are welcome. Nonetheless, we want to make sure that Bob Tail is safe and well-fed.

And that's how writing, even when you want to take a break, attracts strange coincidences. Inside the café where, ten years earlier, Matsu and his band had played, they've set a large table I hadn't noticed from the terrace, and everyone who spoke about Elizabeth Bishop at the seminar is there in this dimly lit retreat. Alan calls for us to join them, we walk over to the table, both of us feeling very unsociable, carrying our cardboard box of leftovers for Bob Tail. It isn't until much later that we'll finally climb over the wall at Hemingway House to visit our vagabond, and find several very plump red cats and a few other anonymous Bob Tails.

But our evening spent with the speakers proves to be unforgettable. Perhaps it's simply the effect of emotions too powerful, like when I dream of Edmund and Elena and think I can hear their voices. I'd been thinking a great deal about Robert Lowell and suddenly I see his ex-wife, Elizabeth Hardwick—so many years after meeting her for the first time at Mary McCarthy's house in Maine; she, like Lowell, is a writer who continues to amaze me today, and she talks to me about Robert as if we had never parted from him.

I evoke my memories of Mary McCarthy, her open-mindedness, her warmth, and suddenly her brother is there among the speakers. He is a famous actor, very handsome, sure of himself, I don't like his insolent attitude when he speaks of his remarkable sister. Perhaps he shares her charm, her sense of humour and fierce tenderness, but he isn't humble, as she was.

It's a shock to feel Mary so close, through such deep blood ties, without her being there. It's almost cruel.

Frank Taylor, ever the same modest friend, winks at me with a glance that seems to say: "I don't like these gatherings any more than you, everyone is so insincere..." I meet Elizabeth Bishop's personable biographer—all these books being written about Elizabeth so long unknown among her peers, would she be proud or sad?

But the words that weigh on my memory become words I want to write: Elizabeth's absence, her death. I'll never again see her at Harvard University, a cigarette in her hand, nor will I see Mary McCarthy preparing to leave for Vietnam, in her army uniform. Jacinthe says: "The night is still young, should we go to the Captain Horn Club and listen to some jazz?"

On our way to the door, we pass Patricia at the bar; superb, like the Queen of the Night, she greets us warmly, surrounded by men. We leave her to her mysterious nightlife and walk into the street; when we reclaim our bicycles, Jacinthe disappears down the road by the cemetery we rode along earlier that evening, the night envelops us, and we could each be alone in the world.

# Notebook 19

*ary and I* first meet Winkie and Gigi during an exhibition of Mary's paintings in Cambridge, in the sixties. The large portraits Mary paints of her family, her friends, capture Winkie's imagination; although she doesn't know Mary at the time, when visiting the gallery with Gigi who is pushing her wheelchair, Winkie is drawn to one of the portraits in the window, as if it were a meeting between one person and another.

The immobility of the faces and bodies in the paintings and the agitation, the movement one senses behind this immobility, achieved by the restless colours on the canvas, this sense of life arrested at the heart of life, is the immobility full of turmoil that Winkie has known ever since she became paralysed at age twenty.

Winkie was born with beauty, wealth, she lived in Hyannis Port, was friends with members of the Kennedy family, practiced the same sports with them; it was a fateful bout of polio that paralysed her spine one summer, immobilizing forever her youth, her entire life. Desperate, her parents sought a companion for her, a man or woman who could help her, prevent her from sinking into despair, someone who could be both a friend and a nurse, caring for her, assisting her day and night, for although she can sit in a wheelchair and use her left hand, she can't live without a respirator, and her life is always in danger.

In Québec, Gigi, who'd been caring for a child about to die of leukemia, read the parents' ad in a newspaper. She replied promptly: if Winkie needs her, she'll be there, she'll come to live with her in the States. Gigi exists, she says, to love others on this Earth, people can count on her presence, her devotion.

Thus begins the long story of the valorous, exemplary friendship between Winkie and Gigi. Mary is touched by the frailty of human beings, her paintings are a reflection, an interrogation of our uneasiness. She paints multiple portraits of her mother, her sister Sarah; her studio in the woods houses all the sketches for these canvasses, the drawings slowly developed in the final painting, then these canvasses are set aside, or slashed in a moment of fury, tossed into the blaze of the municipal dump by the hand that shaped them. One of them will become the portrait of her sick father: a scholar, an intellectual whose concerns are metaphysical; his chin resting on one of his hands, he seems to be wondering what is the meaning of our fleeting passage on this Earth. His eyes are clear blue, he's dressed in a elegant summer suit, his life flits like a dream through his memory, there is no explanation for the anxiety in his gaze except that he is aware of his imminent departure from this life. Dignified and resigned, he is waiting; but through meticulous details, the childhood, the youth of the man stricken with tuberculosis while still young, in the wash of sensual colours that surround the father's pensive head, moments of glory, mere instants perhaps, seem to circle around him in a flood of arrested images: there he is a young boy with his brothers, dressed in his Sunday best for a photograph that seems to come from another century, or later, with his wife and children; his only certainty, as his blue eyes stare out at us, is that this world as he has known it, this lively world, will never return.

It's in Winkie's house in Hyannis Port that one of Mary's portraits will find a home, exercising in the life of Winkie and Gigi its powers of consolation, and although Winkie, like Mary's father, will never be cured, the painting will be a companion in the extremity of her solitude.

Winkie, like Mary's father in the painting, shows unfailing dignity. That summer, several months after Kennedy's assassination, on the beach in front of the Kennedys' house that Winkie can see from her wheelchair on the grand deck that juts out over the sea, Winkie deplores, in her faltering voice contracted by the strain of being connected to the respirator, the absence of the man who was a friend to her, who sometimes came to invite her out or to take her for a walk on the beach. She doesn't refer to the man as "the president of the United States who was just assassinated," but "a very kind man who came to my house as a friend."

Winkie says there are very few adults on the beach this summer, only children playing ball, young people playing tennis; this beach on the Atlantic coast has been draped in mourning, as if in the catastrophic aftermath of a shipwreck. Sometimes Winkie asks Gigi to hold the binoculars to her eyes, perhaps she'll see Ted or Robert Kennedy, in their white shorts, she'll see their hair blowing in the wind, the neck, the nape of the beloved brothers she contemplates from her window or her deck, although the Kennedy compound is some distance from her house, and separated by a fence protected by policemen and security guards. She feels as if today will be the day when the sky is blue and the sea calm, that a young man with a dreamy smile will come to take her out, invite her for a walk on the beach, as if she were walking arm-in-arm with the only man who offers her the miracle of walking again. But it's raining violently and Gigi is worried about Winkie's breathing. Gigi's greatest fear is these coastal gales, all of Nature's violence that could cut off the electricity in the house; this fear is an accurate presentiment, for Winkie will die on a stormy day, at the age of thirty-eight, during a power failure that will deprive her of her breath.

In her letters of exceptional power, as in the autobiography she is writing with Mary's help, in her drawings dominated by pink and green, all the melodious colours, Winkie speaks only of her happiness to be alive, of life as a daily discovery, an adventure despite the terrible confinement of her immobility, brightened by Gigi's friendship and love, and of her astonishment that life is still intact inside her. Never does she evoke her infirmity. In her living room in Hyannis Port, or in Cambridge, when Gigi takes her to the galleries where she buys paintings, Winkie sees painting as a prolongation of her life, just as she sees from her deck in Hyannis Port by the sea, in the desolation of a life lost, the man who to her will always be the luminous visitor, the man who was a lieutenant in the American Navy during World War II, whose bravery she's aware of, but who is first and foremost the man who has the kindness, the simplicity of the humble, and who might come to rest his hand on her wheelchair and say: "Shall we go for a walk on the beach, together, the two of us?"

Although she knows that in this world, where she once knew him handsome and triumphant, this visitor will never return.

## Notebook 20

*Sunday* is not a day of rest in Key West, but it's the day I stop by the Café Billie at noontime to read the newspapers, *USA Today*, the *Miami Herald*, the *New York Times* and the *Key West Citizen* which is a godsend for the citizens of the island. Danny, who's almost a friend, the irreproachable patient waiter, a young man born under the sign of Capricorn, who wears rings in his right ear and who has a Capricorn's wary lucidity and predilection for silence, is reading the horoscope page which has put him in a thoughtful mood. "More financial problems," he says holding his head in his hands beneath the floating air from the fan. "How can that happen to me, when I live alone on my boat, don't have a penny to my name, and spend all my time at work? Oh well, things will improve next week. Capricorns like things that are just beginning, but we get bored really fast... Sometimes I'm not so sure we like life..."

Sunday is also a more carefree day because I know I'll see Patrick at six o'clock in his European-style bar, Square One.

Blond and radiant Patrick, whose indulgent friendship I've enjoyed for the past twelve years, with his quiet tenderness for my friends who are continual subjects of reflection and inspiration, as they were when I wrote, *The Island*, for Jacques Crête and his Montreal theatre company, L'Eskabel.

What would I do without the faces of Danny, Patrick and Barbara who used to dance with Martha Graham's company and is now a taxi driver in Key West, what would become of me if the pessimism or the simple realism of my thoughts on the evolution of humanity were not coloured by the appealing, subtle glow, the objective warmth of their carefree, exuberant summer mood?

Because in my work, it's still winter. The sentence that obsesses me this Sunday is the one I just read here beside Danny who is fending off his boisterous customers. This sentence written by Walt Harrington, is drawn from his book soon to be published under the title: *Crossings: A White Man's Journey into Black America*, from which the *Key West Citizen* has published an excerpt this weekend; in this odyssey of a white writer in black America, I read and reread these words: "In the little town of Marks, Reverend Martin Luther King cried, and from that day on this town in northwestern Mississippi has been called: the town where Martin Luther King cried in 1968, just days before he was assassinated..."

And I can see the town of Marks as the preacher might have seen it that day he was forced to arrive in a rowboat because the rains had flooded and destroyed the town, a fated town, with its few starving Blacks stranded under the rusty tin roofs of their cabins the wind had torn apart, leaving them exposed and shivering in these damp winters where the crops of rice and beans grow precariously, a spindly vegetation of sterile grains growing through the frames of houses, destroyed, crushed by the storm. It is there, passing through the godforsaken village of Street Cotton, with its forlorn cabins and huts built with scraps of salvaged lumber, on his way to the island of the abandoned, in the middle of the peat and the muddy weeds, that the preacher will weep, standing in the rain, hugging the family he found there, a mother, her skinny children slowly being destroyed by cold, sickness, in their shack without windows, without plumbing, disintegrating, sinking, all of them, into the floodwaters with the proliferation of snakes and parasites. There, contemplating the town of Marks and the cabin rotting beneath its rusty roof, that a picture in the weekend newspaper has resurrected from the Mississippi valley where so much black blood has flowed, the distressed preacher will also weep over the cotton and bean plantations where for centuries, their backs burned by the sun, their hands torn by the thorns, his enslaved people have fed the arid soil with their sweat and their tears.

This Sunday the papers will also bring, like a muffled knell tolling in the fog, news of the death of the Japanese novelist, Kobe Abe; another singularly prophetic voice falls silent discreetly, without a fuss. We have lost a great novelist and humanist who, like Moravia, was fascinated by the dark side of human nature, though he also believed that we can be regenerated by the beauty of nature; this man who passionately protected his life, the intensity of his writing haunted by the too rapid modernization of post-war Japan, a conscience with an active role to play in this world, a voice in the wilderness, has ceased to exist, and the news makes me very sad.

d. 1993
(aetat 68)

I'm still carrying, in the pocket of my shorts, at the twilight hour when I go to see Patrick at Square One with a flashlight in the basket on my bicycle so I can get home early enough to write until midnight, both articles clipped from the morning papers: the preacher's tears, the sudden disappearance at age sixty-eight of Japanese novelist Kobo Abe; these treasures that accompany me in the dark lessen my desire to see Patrick and to relax with friends—this sunny day becomes the Sunday of an inner winter where there is no place for peace, for rest.

And suddenly I hear the laughing voices inside the restaurants leading to Square One on Duval Street, with their pink tablecloths and red hibiscus flowers in glasses, waiting for those who'll come for a festive dinner in the mild, night air; this is the hour when every traveller from the icy shores of Germany or Norway watches the steamship *Zenith* or the *Amsterdam* depart as the sun sets over the water, with the passengers blurred in the circles of the portholes; they depart in a turmoil of strident noises and smoke, while the sailboat, *The Predator*, silently slashes the waves, tilting from side to side in the uncertain wind.

Patrick and Barbara, whose long, thin body has preserved from years of training the flexibility, the slightly tense grace of a dancer, are chatting at the bar. Resting her hand on Patrick's arm, Barbara says: "Those of us who have at last found our place, our home port, here, after years of wandering in Puerto Rico, San Francisco—we still haven't seen Europe... Here we are rocked by the Atlantic, never leaving our houses, our cats and our dogs. But what's the sense of going so far afield, Patrick, when I've found in you a friend, and sometimes a father confessor in whom I can confide all my weaknesses, knowing you'll never judge me." When Barbara leans over and tells me that "on this island you mustn't mistake appearances for reality," I feel true respect for her because I sense she's trying to tell me that although she gave up dancing for reasons she prefers not to explain, dance is still inside her. Just as for Patrick, an actor and impersonator, this bar is the stage of a life starting over. "People come here to start over and to heal," says Barbara. "Whether you become a taxi driver or a waiter, you always have another life behind you. And often it's a life in the arts that you've given up, and it's through that resignation that, despite yourself, you learn humility."

On my way home from Square One, from meeting Patrick and Barbara, the flashlight is there to forge my way through the night. Back at my work table, I write these words so I'll never forget them: "Reverend Martin Luther King wept over the town of Marks."

# Notebook 21

*What was Barbara's intellectual background* when Mary and I met her at the Tallahassee airport on that dreary winter day in 1964, after many days of fasting in the Southern jail where she had been detained with other American pacifists in her non-violent fight against racism and global nuclear armament? First, a scholarly mind eager for knowledge, a poet who wrote her first poems at the age of fifteen, a writer. This woman who is so hurt by injustice done to others seems to have suddenly chosen non-violent action out of spiritual necessity and heartfelt compassion.

As she walks toward us in the worn green coat that served as her blanket in jail, Barbara is so emaciated, has lost so much weight, Mary bursts into tears when she sees her; I, who had never seen Barbara, except in Mary's drawings and in photographs, am shocked by her skeletal thinness and the harsh treatment she suffered in prison. I recognize from Mary's drawings the romantic model with the often anxious brown eyes, her head cocked, pensive over a body too tall, the hair she cuts herself falls in bangs over her forehead, then straight in a short page-boy.

In her search for truth of a superior order that has now become, when I first see her in the Tallahassee airport, the object of her entire life, Barbara has already written extensively on American society in the fifties and sixties. One of her articles, published in the review *Liberation*, expresses her own liberation: *One Woman's Journey towards Truth: Chronicle of a Woman's Liberation*. In a long essay on American cinema in the forties, she analyses, through the heroes of war films, the notion of collective violence, a subject that gives her no respite. At the same time, her interest in the arts has taken many forms; she has studied literature and theatre as a student at Bennington College, where her drawing teacher was George Grosz; she has taught theatre, been project director in a New York arts centre, assistant editor to writer Bessie Breuer; she has written an essay on *Hamlet* in which her feminist preoccupations are already evident, and it was after a trip to India that she began to read Gandhi; it is Gandhi's works that guide her towards non-violent action as a means of pacifist protest against racism and the Vietnam War.

As early as 1960, she had already visited Cuba and talked to Castro, become a disciple of Gandhi and met with members of the Non-Violent Action Committee; in 1961, she was arrested with her friends from the International Peace Brigade during a demonstration held as part of a conference against atomic weapons.

On this winter morning when I see her for the first time in this Florida airport where police officers are watching from a distance—I feel as if this tight surveillance is very close to us, although the police are not there for Barbara, but for a criminal on the run—her frightful thinness attracts a great deal of attention. Our unhappiness for her is not shared by Barbara, she is proud of her strength and serene after the battle, for she now sees her life as a constant struggle for the creation of a better society. During her incarceration in the Birmingham jail, she wrote her book *Prison Notes* which will be read by future generations of pacifists and non-violent resisters; it is also the diary of a revolutionary, a mystic who believes in prayer and fasting, and the story of an experience of solidarity with other militant comrades, who countered deprivation with love.

In her books, Barbara often speaks of the progress that one individual's consciousness can achieve, she says we are on this Earth to work without respite on ourselves. This rigorous concentration is obvious when I see her spend entire days writing, sitting straight at her typewriter, stopping occasionally at midday to drink a drop of port when her strength fails. Her work space is overflowing with newspapers, books on Cuba; during these years in the sixties, when she answers the telephone, it's to receive news about a friend just released from jail, about fellow-militants fasting for disarmament in Washington: Ray Robinson, a black militant who accompanied her on a Peace March for Cuba, is, along with Martin Luther King, her emotional link to the black community; they talk to each other almost daily. By a cruel twist of fate, Ray will be killed by an Indian at Wounded Knee, during a peaceful demonstration in defense of native rights. This disappearance, like that of Martin Luther King, is a source of immense sorrow in Barbara's life. The day seems unreal in this Florida airport where Blacks are still denied access to public areas reserved for Whites, the place seems cursed, the suffering on Barbara's face etched in the rays of the tropical sun; it is here in the Florida Keys, on the sandy beaches, that Barbara will regain her strength, without ever truly recovering her health because the fasting, too severe and excessive, has seriously upset her metabolism. Although I don't realize it then, and it will take several years, it's at this time she will begin to die of the ovarian cancer that will finally claim her in her house in Sugarloaf, where her rowboat awaits her in the canal.

This evolution, the progression of a conscience attuned to the world's pain, to its evils and injustices, will be Barbara's legacy long after her death, long after the excursions in the rowboat have ended; her writing, her books prolong her work, and nothing, as she always said, has been achieved, except that a single conscience is quietly growing, perfecting itself somewhere in total darkness.

# Notebook 22

*In these summers of light* on the dunes of Cape Cod, the limpid light that reflects the brightness of the ocean waves, on these long July and August days when you can still stroll on the beach at night, on these beaches where horses occasionally gallop with their haughty riders, the painters come down from the dunes and set up their canvas stools in the sand near the water. There's Mary, off to one side, painting a marsh; there'll be the marsh painted on a drizzly day, the marsh painted in autumn and the state of mind of the painter in the maturity of her art. And there are the oyster and clam shells in paintings by Mary and her friend Leonid who once gave her lessons in her studio in New York.

When they come from New York, from Vermont or Connecticut, to spend their vacation painting the light of Cape Cod, the painters say they are going to the sea; they dream for months of this journey where they'll be alone with the ocean, marine life and their drawing tables, their wooden easels and the canvasses they take wherever they go.

In the cottages they rent—always facing the sea—Diana paints a red chair beside a window overlooking the bay at sunset. For many years this red chair and the unlimited space that frames the watercolour painted in exquisite strokes will symbolize for me the solitude of the painter—the chair, in the middle of an expanse of water and sky, is the image of Diana herself facing the journey to the gates of the infinite, on this sea with no end in sight, no limit, since the foam of its waves blends into the sky. It is death that's hiding in the distance, yet already feels so close.

White shells, bleached by the tides, a crab with its legs arched, painted by Leonid, are images of human skeletons beneath the earth and dust that covers buried bodies. But, for Leonid, the sea, and its vast enigma, is also perpetual life and the hope of all birth. When Mary draws a dead bird on the shore, a moment of effervescence, of life freezes beneath her pencil or pen. Years later, the small bird killed by the storm, drawn in brown ink on a sketch pad, still has in its half-closed eye a twinkle of life.

Many years later, in a country house, although Leonid has been gone for years, his large paintings bring back the shining seas of summer evenings on Cape Cod; at the bottom of the painting, at the very edge, a slight figure, of little weight, little flesh, is watching or simply passing by, like us, a life easily swept away, obliterated by the waves of an inescapable death. That alone remains undeniable, our mortality, our precarious existence under this sun, near this sea which, unlike us, will not disappear.

In Key West, my friends, the islanders, often plan to go to sea. The heavy schedule that sometimes keeps them at work until late at night, in their jazz clubs, in the refuge of a room where they write their books, or others, like Mazu, compose their music, forces them to postpone these departures, but whenever one of them says: "We'll charter a big boat, we'll go fishing in the middle of the ocean," there's always something magical about the invitation. A new light is cast on our everyday duties and obligations, and more distant frontiers appear.

At last, it's the departure day we've talked about so often, the story told before we lived it, and, barely out of bed, we're all on the deck of *Don't Miss the Boat*. We're there at dawn, groggy and forlorn, before the skippers arrive with the fishing rods and the bait. We huddle together surrounded by pelicans flapping their wings, grey and yellow as dirty clothes. Mazu rubs his eyes and says, stifling a yawn, that with such a cloudless blue sky the wind will be light and our boat stable. The boat is already rocking in the roar of the motor. Jacinthe and I glance at Mazu not really believing him, Jacinthe wearing a fisherman's cap and sunglasses, her hair pulled back with an elastic under her hat, both of us wishing we had never considered this excursion on the water, hiding behind our dark glasses. We must look as if we're in a foul mood, and suddenly, we're off; the earlybirds, Pauline and Renaud, are cheerful on the deck, Pauline's face barely visible beneath her broad straw hat; Renaud, the most exuberant of us all, is barechested in the sun, his jean shorts rolled up above his knees, his hair blowing in the wind, he asks Mazu if anyone lives on the bouquet of islands the boat is passing. Yes, says Mazu, there's always the odd shrimp fisherman on these islands, or a hermit, a woman or a man, who's taken shelter there. Mazu points out the shrimp boat, alone in the middle of the sea, its shape, with the sails billowing over the water, is that of a butterfly.

We pull away from the coast, leaving behind the string of islands and the sailboats tilting into the wind; the vegetation fades away, until the Australian pines and mangroves are mere traces of colour in an aquarelle blurred by water, and suddenly, with a hoarse shudder, the boat stops on the high seas. This is when the fishermen cast their nylon lines, spinning their reels amid cries and gasps; from these waters riled by the dancing lures will surge the innocent creatures with pierced eyes, and fins bathed in blue and purple blood. For a long while, the red snapper, the fish with yellow wings called the yellowtail, the catfish, the kingfish, transferred to a pail, will thrash their tails, their fins, their gilded scales glinting in the rosy water, until we finally hear the painful murmur, a plaintive almost human sigh, of their last breath.

But the catch is good, Renaud, Mazu and Pauline are jolly, their faces tanned by the sun and the wind; they'll stand in the same cloud of pelicans and wait for the skippers to cut the fish into filets, the harvest of the sea from which Mazu will prepare us a banquet that evening.

But in the middle of the ocean, while casting our lines into the sea, each of us felt, in the luminosity of the water, that we are of little weight, of little flesh at the gates of infinity, like the figure in Leonid's painting; each of us caught a glimpse, in a fleeting yet voluptuous frisson, of what it would be like, the last breath, the one that catches us fluttering, still hooked on the lure of life.

## Notebook 23

*It's a foggy night* on the coast as the woods and lakes roll by, the outlines of the bays emerge in the blue almost warm mist of a summer night in Maine, and we approach Castene and Mary McCarthy's home; at times the fog is so dense we think we've lost our way, and when we finally arrive, it's so late everyone is standing by the fireplace waiting for us in the aroma of a crispy meal that has been ready since nightfall. There they are, they come to greet us, glass in hand, in the yellow living room with the high cedar bookcases, Mary and her husband, James, Robert Lowell, Elizabeth Hardwick, all militant writers, they send letters to the editor, they protest against the war in Vietnam and I hear these voices united in their moderation, their controlled anger, condemning the bombing of Hanoi and its outlying areas, and the destruction by American aviators of the country's plantations and forests.

When they explode, Agent Orange bombs spray thousands of murderous drops destroying the forests of bamboo, of rare hardwood, the fields where neither rice nor manioc nor sweet potatoes will grow for another twenty years.

As I write this notebook, I can see Mary McCarthy's face, I can hear her voice, in the yellow living room where <u>Robert Lowell</u> suddenly confessed that he'd been suffering from serious depression since the beginning of this war; I can almost hear his wife's voice gently reminding him that he'd always been plagued by this latent depression, ever since he began writing.

The poet, slim and wiry in his tight jeans, is attractive and shy, he smokes nervously, speaks very little, his soul is heavy with secrets he cannot share with us. Only his closest friends know the depths of the depression and the quest for serenity this man faces every day, in his life, and in his work where he attempts to illuminate his exacerbated vision of the world, and that's when writing weighs so heavily: while he writes, he says, bombs are destroying Hanoi.

Robert will die of a heart attack in a taxi cab in New York, on his way home from a trip to Ireland. Almost thirty years later, when, among the writers invited to a seminar on Elizabeth Bishop and her work, I run into Elizabeth Hardwick in Key West, Robert Lowell, this tall young man with his awkward gestures, still seems to be standing at her side, as he was in the yellow living room of an old New England farmhouse, at Mary McCarthy's; suddenly the memory of him is so present, the memory of the majesty of Robert's pain, that we look at each other, Elizabeth and I, devastated, aware of the absurdity of the poet's death, in a taxi cab, before he can join his friends and family who've been waiting for him during this long absence from which, perhaps she had sensed, he'd never return.

That same evening in Key West, the appearance of Kevin McCarthy, Mary's brother who bears such a strong physical resemblance to her, both delights and shocks me, for he is still alive while she no longer is, and there is power in men's longevity. Later Frank will tell me that Kevin is eighty years old, but that evening he looks sixty, and his youthful air offends me; so late in life Kevin still possesses the confidence of men who remain young and handsome so long, he has a young wife, young children, and his sister barely older than he, whose vitality was so fertile and innovative, is no longer with us to pursue her life of creativity.

When I see him, she is the one I miss, but who can say whether these two beings don't complement each other even if I cannot grasp the mysterious lineage of the bond that unites them?

One sunny morning in Key West, I have a fleeting insight into the nature of this bond when I least expect it, on Whitehead Street where nonchalant dogs sprawl in the middle of the street, oblivious to the black schoolchildren walking home from school and the frantic race of college students on their motorcycles. On Whitehead Street, on my way to the post office, Annie Dillard, the American writer whose fine book, *An American Childhood*, I've just discovered, stops her yellow car beside my bicycle and invites me to follow her to Rollie McKenna's house, to meet her little girl of eight. "You have to meet my daughter, Rosie. Rollie babysat for her this morning while I was working, I'm going to pick her up...You'll see, Rosie is an amazing child." But for me, this sparkling morning is a fierce morning, I confide in Annie, I confess my anxiety about writing these notebooks, I also tell her how disturbing I find these memories of the destruction of Vietnam. Annie repeats: "You have to meet Rosie, she's an amazing child..."

It's at Rollie's house, near the blue pool where Rosie is swimming in the aura of her own glow as sparkling as the sun and water, that I'll be struck by another revelation: I suddenly notice among some recent photographs Rollie has just hung on the wall of her studio, after her exhibition of photographs of Elizabeth Bishop in the Martello Tower Museum, a photograph that wasn't on the wall a few days earlier, that of Kevin McCarthy, whose face this time, as Rollie, physiognomist of character as well as of faces, reveals, is truly that of his sister, with her piercingly intelligent eyes and her humanity.

In one of her poems, Elizabeth Bishop writes that the world is "minute, vast and clear"—looking at that photograph of Mary's brother, the world did seem a very small place, though very clear and very vast, where we constantly encounter the same faces, the same voices, and although we sometimes think death has erased these faces, silenced these voices, they seem to have been imprinted on us for all eternity.

# Notebook 24

*Leonid paints the light* that descends on the bay in the evening, he paints the unique light of Cape Cod that has a touch of melancholy even on sunny summer days. His wife, Sylvia Marlowe, is the harpsichordist the New York critics compared to Wanda Landowska in the sixties. They are two inseparable companions, united by the same passion for their art, music and painting. They have already reached the threshold of old age when I visit them with Mary in their New York attic furnished primarily with musical instruments and canvasses that devour the space. Leonid— whom Sylvia, with her natural spontaneity, calls Coco, for it's Leonid who determines Sylvia's teaching and practice schedule—is preparing an exhibition of his Cape Cod landscapes, but he is calm, as he stands contemplating his canvasses, wearing his jaunty black beret. Sylvia flutters around him, smoking constantly.

Leonid's kind eyes glance at her occasionally in adoration, the expression in Leonid's eyes is loving, like the eyes of a dog. "Coco, where are my cigarettes?" Sylvia asks. "If I've run out, you'll have to go down and buy me some...Where's my sheet music? What would I do without you, Coco?"

Sylvia is soon to give a recital at Carnegie Hall and Leonid, who bites his tongue, docilely obeying his wife's orders, fetching her cigarettes, her sheet music, is concerned that Sylvia has resumed her harpsichord recitals too soon after a recent bout of illness. Gently he suggests, "Isn't it a bit too soon for this Carnegie Hall recital, you're still not cured and you've already started to work..."

Sylvia replies in an authoritarian voice that she feels well enough to perform, and how could she go on living without music? And we hear, in this New York attic, the passionate music Sylvia plays, the music of Poulenc, of Manuel de Falla, works commissioned by the Polish harpsichordist Wanda Landowska. These harpsichord works by Poulenc and Manuel de Falla will be part of Sylvia's recital a few days later.

Meanwhile, according to the same newspapers advertising Sylvia's upcoming concert, New York has discovered the Living Theatre. It's Barbara's fascination for anarchistic art that leads me to attend several performances by this extraordinary troupe she refers to as a community of activist actors; Barbara has practiced nonviolent action with the two founding members of the Living Theatre, Julian Beck and Judith Malina. But beneath the apparent anarchy, the unruly performance of the actors who roll across the stage in costumes that look like ragged burlap coats or brown wool tunics tied at the waist with a rope, their pale bodies sticking out of their rags, in a chaotic chorus of cries and song, it's the discipline, the rigour that strikes me. Here, what Artaud called "the theatre of cruelty" has become the theatre of unbearable reality, the reality of oppression, racism, war.

The actors are no longer separate from the spectators, we are what they are performing, they stomp around us, invading the entire space which suddenly becomes the stage of world politics and all the calamities of history.

The Living Theatre imposes its art of protest, nothing can escape our memory, or our lethargic conscience. We stand face to face with victims of the concentration camps, and those of the Vietnam War and its bombs. In his attic studio in New York, Leonid paints the vast immovable blue sky. He tells Sylvia we must maintain peace of heart. He applies damp compresses to Sylvia's eyes when she's played the harpsichord too long, and urges her to rest more. She ignores him and Coco is put off when Sylvia, visibly annoyed, insists that she doesn't need him. But it's the day before the concert and Sylvia wants to know if her black silk dress is still at the cleaners, and how can Coco be so negligent, forgetting her dress.

Then it's the evening of Sylvia's concert at Carnegie Hall. Leonid, Mary and I watch the frail musician playing the music of Poulenc. Leonid's kind dog-like eyes are full of concern. Why did his wife agree to give this recital? The blasé, merciless critics won't hesitate to underline the shortcomings of her performance, for, pained, Leonid can feel her fingers hesitate over the keyboard of the harpsichord, even if Sylvia is playing with the same impetuous conviction as before, when she gave concerts throughout the United States and Europe; tonight the critics will regret having compared her to Wanda Landowska, they'll forget the quality of her dazzling genius and they'll show no pity for the musician whose health is failing.

Proud in her black dress, her hair gathered in a chignon at the nape of her neck, Sylvia plays, but as she leans over the keyboard, darkness falls, her fingers slide limply over the notes that seem to elude her. Suddenly Sylvia forgets those who are listening to her, watching her, there's the sound of coughing in the concert hall, a ripple of dissatisfied sighs, Sylvia is alone as she sets out on the dark journey of old age. She thinks about the woman who was such a source of inspiration, the impeccable Wanda Landowska who from childhood mastered the harpsichord, and who would devote her entire life to this instrument, through her work as a teacher and her concerts of contemporary music.

Sylvia is distressed that her fingers are suddenly playing so badly—as if her hands had been paralysed by the cold—this music by Poulenc that she knows so well, this fluid, free-flowing music. As for Manuel de Falla, how dare she attack it when she feels overcome by this new sensation of impotence?

There's a long silence in the concert hall, we don't dare glance at the New York critics who are already standing up to leave, before the end of the concert. Leonid lowers his black beret over his brow. It's wintertime, a cold wind blows through the streets, grey characters in rags who could be part of a Living Theatre production prowl around the garbage pails on respectable 44th Street. Dressed in her black dress under a fur coat, Sylvia walks home, on Leonid's arm.

# Notebook 25

*It's a time of long visits* in a house without electricity in Maine, a house lit by the cheery glow of oil lamps in the evening, austere summers spent writing a novel inspired by my friends Jack and Robert from Cambridge, a short novel about social responsibility, personal distress, it's the birth of someone unknown to me before meeting Jack, my student friend from Cambridge who would be destroyed by drugs, and Robert, the young black writer forever maimed by the cruelty of racism—it's the birth of David Sterne. My friends live again in the hero of this novel, a character whose youth was shattered.

Mary is absorbed all day in her sketchbooks, with her bamboo pen she draws the fields scorched by the sun, the apple trees and their cool shadows: on the white pages of her sketchbooks India ink captures the shapes and images of the beauty of nature.

The atrocious war continues. Jack has become a conscientious objector, a draft dodger who fled to Canada; unable to adapt, he returns to Cambridge where he resumes his drifting and his abuse of alcohol and mescaline.

Robert has written an autobiographical novel rejected by his publisher; in his novel, Robert writes about earning a living from prostitution in the streets of New York. The novel will never be published.

As I write my novel, Jack's and Robert's faces blend into a single tragic figure, that of a generation doomed, by war, the war in Vietnam, and segregation which has already claimed so many victims, to an untimely demise, premature exhaustion.

Occasionally during these summers, Barbara comes to rest; it's shortly before she leaves on a pacifist mission to Vietnam, shortly before we see her picture in the newspapers when she is attacked by soldiers while demonstrating with friends in Saigon.

The appearance of well-known artists breaks the isolation of the silent countryside. Among the artists and writers who retreat to Maine in the summertime, I'll see John Cage create his music at the Skowhegan School, he says we can all participate in his constructions, that we too could invent unlimited sounds; he experiments with diverse tones, percussion instruments, radio static, microphones, all the objects found in the concert hall which is a barn overlooking pastures where sheep graze peacefully; the most humble objects of mechanized life are transformed into a barbaric concrete symphony that at once shocks and captivates our senses. A sound as harsh as a door slamming, paired with the sound of water, the high-pitched song of a flute, transports us, taking us to the spellbinding sonorous regions John Cage has made his domain.

During this concert, I'm preoccupied by the style of my novel, I'd like to hear the voice of the text, undoubtedly a broken voice, like John Cage's music; the style won't be conventional, for when I think of Jack and Robert, of the crises in those two lives, I can feel myself shudder with the blows, the vertiginous sense of being, that inhabited them both. Robert survived his disappointments, we no longer see him walking in the dunes, his arm protectively around Jane's shoulders, for ever since Jane lost all her hair during her treatment for breast cancer, they are no longer seen taking their long walks; discouraged by the publishers' rejections, Robert has withdrawn yet he perseveres in his writing. But what will become of him when Jane is no longer at his side?

Sometimes a dark fire shines in Robert's eyes seeming to say "I hate you all." When we meet in the streets of Wellfleet or Truro, he doesn't speak to me, doesn't even seem to see me.

I rewrite my novel several times, giving the writing a restless, feverish tone; the music of the text is that of a fragmented, jagged poem, all fits and starts and dull thuds, like the lives of Jack and Robert. Michel Rameau's jump from the belltower of the boarding school chapel, his silent, wordless leap, is Jack's leap into the void from the tenth floor of a Boston hotel, the tireless persecution of David Sterne by the police, is the story of Robert, cornered and persecuted by white people, there is no respite in his life, not even the oasis of intellectual life he thought he'd found by writing books.

Jack leaves a note behind. "I'm taking off, it's too hard and no one wants to help me in my rehabilitation, nor do I see any end to the war. Goodbye." Yet, thanks to the militants, the war did come to an end, and Jack could have enjoyed years of happiness, going to live in the country, getting married, raising a family, as he'd always hoped, but the flower child, the wild-spirited hippie, got lost along the wayside.

The time has come to return to Wellfleet. My novel is finished at last, although the lives of Jack and Robert continue to weigh heavily on me. Through the pine forests of Wellfleet and Truro, along the clutch of winding roads and paths where mushrooms grow, I ride my bike to Provincetown, a joyful town humming with the love of boys for each other, alive with their advances, their tender promiscuity, in the streets, in the hotel rooms where curtains flutter in the sea breeze, a town of sexual liberation in those days, because moral strictness is relaxing its grip and everyone feels free to celebrate his or her way of loving and living with a freedom so new it smacks of wild, intoxicating adventure. I'd only known Provincetown in the winter, visiting with Mary her painter and poet friends who lived hidden behind their closed shutters—now the deserted shores have become summer beaches where young people in love lie in the sun, and in the eyes of some, one can still detect the doubts and candour of adolescence.

And now, many years later, the streets of Provincetown no longer ring with the confident joviality of those voices, those healthy voices unconcerned with health; under the same blue sky that sheltered those sensuous holidays, a deadly silence has seized the bodies of these gods resting or sleeping on the beaches. The list of those who have disappeared is longer than they care to count. The wind of the plague has blown this way.

# Notebook 26

*P*rince Alexander. When Nina pronounces his name for the first time in the living room with blue draperies where Elena entertains her guests in her house in Wellfleet, he is already a mythical character for me. Nina is sitting on the sofa beside Elena who is attempting to comfort her. Nina, whose past also belongs to the distant dynasties of the Romanovs, is a small, frail woman with stooped shoulders; she is confiding in Elena who listens to her material worries with the respectful concern she feels for her exiled friends, Nina and her husband Paul, a Georgian prince, now stranded in the woods of Wellfleet with their desolate memories.

Nina says: "Our cousin Alexander is coming to visit soon, he mustn't realize how dire our circumstances are. Paul had the walls of the house painted pink, to save face..." Elena replies in French, with her Germanic accent, "Dear Nina, you shouldn't lower yourself, doing humiliating chores for others, let me help you..." The two women use the formal *vous* when speaking to each other, in a tone of mutual deference.

Nina straightens her shoulders and says, "You alone understand, Elena, how hard it is to muster the courage and dignity we need to go on living..."

At the time Paul has undertaken a fictional biography of Czar Nicholas II Alexandrovitch; he writes in a freezing room, chewing on his pencils, staring at walls the colour of gumdrops. What kind of a man was the last emperor of Russia? Paul's admiration as a child for the czar, who cast his shadow over the kingdom and its magnificence, this admiration that was so sincere has faded; speaking to his writer friends, Paul refers to himself as "a mouse who wants to give birth to an elephant."

Paul understands that the dream has become a nightmare, a burden on his conscience; the man he revered as a little boy was an inept, reactionary ruler, responsible for great repression and numerous massacres, including the massacre historians consider to be one of the cruelest and most cowardly of all, that of hundreds of striking workers in the salt mines of Siberia.

The winter dampness penetrates the house without a fireplace where Paul writes every morning, and in the afternoon he takes long walks on the deserted beach with his dog, Noukfa, who runs along behind him barking; never has Paul been so sad, for he is poor and his wife, this woman of great nobility, has been reduced to cleaning other people's houses; the czar once admired now cloaks him in a cloud of blood as he braves the wind off the Atlantic, his raincoat pulled over his head. But perhaps all that will soon change because Nina's cousin, Prince Alexander, who is, they say, a kind young man who has read all the books, is coming to visit.

This story could have taken place ages ago, in the world of Gogol's books, and yet some of the characters are still alive.

One weekend evening, John Malcolm Brinnin, the intimate biographer of Truman Capote, the rigorous poet capable of understanding Dylan Thomas and the secret of his madness, calls me several times, almost demanding that I leave my seclusion to meet "some surprising friends—you simply must join us, since you didn't even attend the seminar on Elizabeth Bishop... and especially tonight... come around seven o'clock to the garden at the Audubon House, we'll be expecting you..."

When I arrive, not even the affable gallantry of my friend John Malcolm can put me at ease, since I'm not used to attending dinners with patrons and bankers; they are, however, all very nice and interested in my situation, that of the solitary woman writer whose books are undoubtedly among the ten million books in the public library of New York, their city, in their bookstores and their language, but there are so many writers in this world, they can't read them all. The cocktail hour is relaxing, white tablecloths glow in the lamplight under the tree with the orchids. Margaret, a faithful reader who is almost eighty, tells me: "You used to have two readers, they were my friends, you met them at my house years ago... Unfortunately they are no longer with us..." Then the lady sighs impatiently: "How much longer are they going to make us wait for dinner, I'm starving..." Since everyone's name is written on a card, Margaret is eagerly looking for her place.

And here's my place, chosen by fate, or the fairy who guided John Malcolm's hand or that of his hosts: I am sitting to the left of Prince Alexander and in no time we are talking about Paul and Nina, who were his cousins and who, like my two elusive white-haired readers, are "no longer with us," says the prince, his title clearly written on the card indicating his place, "Prince Alexander Romanov."

There's no point in trying to understand the mystery that links the prince to the poet John Malcolm since we quickly find ourselves in the world where characters are invented, or unexpectedly discovered by the novelist, the poet; John Malcolm found the prince and he'll invent him tomorrow in his books.

Alexander is very tall, he has a dreamy expression and green eyes, his voice is charming when he talks to Margaret about his preference for the fashionable clubs in London and Paris where people of his class gather. A woman chokes while eating; I noticed her dazzling entrance in the garden; a waiter takes her by the arm, and leads her to his car, "to drive her to the emergency ward;" the woman disappears in the car, in a glitter of jewels and silk. It's strange that no one, even much later in the evening, except John and me has inquired: "What became of the woman who choked during dinner?"

It's true that Prince Alexander has read all the books, he is kind, as Paul and Nina said, his is an aerial kindness—suddenly he turns to me and says with a gravity I didn't suspect of him, "My cousins Paul and Nina suffered a great deal in their youth...Where is that woman who choked while eating, who was so charming?"

# Notebook 27

*God is love.* I read these words on the blackboard nailed to the wall of the Methodist church on Fleming Street, as a tornado-force wind bends and tears at the palm trees whose heavy branches lay strewn on the sidewalks; the wind is so strong my bicycle can hardly move forward toward the pink Spanish-style building of the church which, at this hour and in this storm that sends the ocean waves crashing over the boardwalks, is uninhabited, the doors and stained glass windows sealed over its silence like blind eyes.

On Sunday, during her sermon, Pastor Esther Robinson will pronounce these words amid the urgent clamour of prayer and song: "God is Love." No one dares set foot outside today when the electricity has been off for hours. Only one little girl with her long hair in braids plows down Fleming Street on her rollerskates, valiantly swinging her arms in her struggle against the cold wind. As she passes me, she says "I'm brave but I'm getting nowhere, the wind keeps pushing me backwards."

In 1963, Barbara denounced the crimes committed by white people against the black citizens of Birmingham: schools were burned, a church was bombed with black children inside, sacrificial victims of these criminal acts. In 1993, the 1923 massacres in the city of Rosewood are remembered in the newspapers, and the old shame comes back to haunt us. Sometimes it's a surviving witness who recalls the events: he saw, he says, the assassins arrive in the night, they lynched, killed almost the entire black population of Rosewood, and today these assassins deny their crimes. Certainly we're on the threshold of hell when such crimes can go unpunished, even years later.

In the novel I've been working on for years—and I don't regret the frightful amount of time writing robs from life, its joys and pleasures, for each detail of the novel must be carefully treated and this task is very demanding—Pastor Robinson becomes Pastor Jeremy who also says in his sermons that God is love. The innocence, the humility of Pastor Jeremy prevents him from looking back to the past and the murders of Birmingham and Rosewood, but his children, the children of Bahama Street, Carlos and Venus, are haunted by these murders at night. In their dreams, the white horsemen of the Apocalypse perpetrate their crimes, and Venus and Carlos see their schools, their colleges and churches go up in flames, over and over again.

I tell Cynthia in the chilly shade of a café terrace where we go to sit together that she has given me part of my character Venus, for whom the massacres of Rosewood are still present, even in her subconscious that tries to flee this reality through drugs; Cynthia tells me it was her younger brother's downfall, escaping through cocaine and crack, that she also went through this indescribable descent into the abyss, but that she learned to defend herself better than her brother and her cousins who are now in jail. First, you have to be strong, she says, feel a merciless strength inside yourself, and never give in to others, you have to be implacable but conserve a mask of sweetness. Cynthia is wearing a red wool dress, she's provocative and sensual, she says with a broad smile of intelligent irony: "It took me two hours to read your book *Deaf to the City*, so it must have taken you two hours to write it; seriously, I feel the same way as you about this world we live in, I wish I could write everything I think and my vision of the world would be very tough... But you know how much I love life... The true injustice is that we're sending soldiers to Somalia while here at home, in my own neighbourhood, black children still haven't been vaccinated... That's the Rosewood scandal of today... I provide dates for people who don't have any, I bring silent bodies to life... Is that so bad? I'm not illegal yet... and all my money will go to the children. The people who judge me should do as much..."

Cynthia, so alive, rebellious, against all religious and moral repression—Cynthia could be Venus, the daughter of Pastor Jeremy in my novel, this pastor who loves God and his many children but who constantly reproaches his daughters for their beauty, the opulence of their bosoms under the sheer fabric of their summer dresses. Cynthia dances as she speaks, men swarm around her, around her languorous voice, the rings and bangles flashing on her dark skin. Among the presents, the packages she'll transport in the basket of her bicycle—how will she manage, she asks laughing—she's holding on a hanger the scoop-neck silk blouse she'll wear that evening at a party where she'll sing the blues; she also has a French class at three o'clock. After all, doesn't a girl in an escort agency have to know everything, learn everything?

she asks, and Cynthia's refinement is so natural, her desire to learn so raw and confident I sense that she is about to defeat the shadows of Rosewood.

God is love, God is my guide, I see these words for the second time as I push my bicycle home along Truman Street, clutching my handlebars with both hands in the wind that howls and sweeps away trees and pieces of roof, everything in its path; as I approach the sea I see a young man staggering under a huge wooden cross in which nails have been hammered, and it's in the midst of these nails, on the cross, that I read the words, God is Love, and the young man under the cross that is crushing him, alone in the storm and the wind, cries and wails, "Every day I walk ten miles with my cross on my back, only God can still save you, I'm telling you but you won't listen to me, God is Love, could you give me two dollars, please..."

The wretched boy is right, no one is listening to him. Only the wind can be heard whining in the empty streets.

# Notebook 28

*rances Shannahan begins practicing* sculpture at age sixty. Her friends are painters, writers: Mary is studying her self-portraits; Diana is drawing in tortured black pencil strokes a tree whose branches were twisted by the storm, the strokes of the drawing are precise and firm, as if the tree with the torn trunk held us inside its misshapen branches, in the chaos of its sudden upheaval; Laetitia who lives in Italy is painting the light of the Mediterranean on the white houses, its softness, the indolence of its colours in her landscapes of Naples and Capri. Frances observes, listens to her friends; although sculpture exerts a latent fascination in her life, for years she'll say humbly, "I'm not an artist like the rest of you, I like living in the country with my dogs, I have no particular vocation, except to understand those who are creative, can a creative woman simply survive?"

Although the feminist revolution is still in its hesitant beginnings in the sixties, Frances expresses her outrage at seeing the works of women painters, sculptors, still go unrecognized and ignored. She says, "Even the critics in the *New York Times* barely mention Berthe Morisot, they only talk about the men who influenced her, Manet, Corot... when she's the one who invented the explosion of nuances and tones in intimist painting..."

It's in the company of Frances, and her friend Diana, that I'll first see a woman conduct an orchestra at the college in Brattleboro, where, in the cool fall evenings in Vermont, sitting on the straight-backed chairs of parish halls, we'll listen to *L'Enfance du Christ*, Berlioz's sacred trilogy, the *Te Deum*, the *Requiem*, this modern, revolutionary music so long misunderstood by audiences; for many years it was considered disastrous music, and suddenly it's a woman conductor who makes us embrace it in our hearts, it's Blanche Moïse leading a group of musicians who are almost all men, it's this woman of sixty, like Frances, at once virile and blessed with an expressive tenderness that charms the musicians, who uplifts us, allows us to appreciate sublime music in which she has perceived the truly feminine sensitivity.

During the intermission at one of these concerts, Frances walks beside me under a canopy of pine trees; I glance at her, chainsmoking feverishly, her face with its classical features is spattered with freckles, she is wearing a green velvet jacket. Her tall boyish body leans towards me, I can smell the strong cigarettes she smokes as she says: "I should just imitate Blanche, if I'm not satisfied with my life... Sometimes Diana's success hurts me... That's unhealthy, I should just start sculpting and I'll feel better. After all, Blanche had the courage to surprise us all... Everyone kept telling her a woman could never conduct an orchestra like a man... She decided not to listen to anyone... I'll do the same thing... And we'll see..."

And it's with this resolve that Frances tackles the raw materials that resist her, granite, marble, bronze, metal.

The granite, the marble are unwieldy, the shapes remain captive so long, their inertia terrifies Frances who runs her agile fingers over this seemingly immobile material. And suddenly the stubborn forehead of a sheep, the tips of aggressive horns appear, ears, and the foreheads of uncertain animals prehistoric or faithful to an ancient memory of the world, everything is there, life, its pulse, its impatient breath.

Stone is heavy to transport. Frances drives to the quarries, the caves, in a truck; but her boyish body is the fragile body of a woman when it comes to carrying such heavy materials. Frances watches the blocks she has to lift every day fall to her feet, the blocks of still formless stone, which despite their heaviness will take the shape of surprising winged creatures. Forms one can imagine from the brush of Cocteau, of Picasso, in the vibrant Vermont air.

Suddenly doves or owls appear, their shapes often undefined; when Frances feels her fingers seized by the anxiety of doubt, an effort that would be awkward, she leaves the piece unfinished, she surrenders it to her anger, her defeat, in a field, a garden. Life springs up everywhere. A cat appears beneath a cedar tree, a lion, a frog, smiling animals stand in the grass, on the lawn we cut today or beside a pile of weeds in the sun.

Frances sculpts day and night.

Frances will die in a moment of distraction, in a stupid car accident in the hills of Vermont where she finally found peace of mind in the resistant art of sculpture. Out of the stone, bronze, metal, human forms began to emerge, a worried smile appearing from the earth, a face, its broad eyelids lowered over the silence of grey stone, eroded by the rain, because Frances worked outside, in the fresh air, surrounded by the trees and the animals who inspired her art. Today, in those same fields of Vermont, in that garden, one can still see her sculptures among the weeds, or standing in the snow and the wind.

When I walk with Diana in these woods, I can hear Frances' soul breathing in the stone, and I think, "where are you now, why did you leave so soon?"

# Notebook 29

She invites me to her summer house on Cape Cod, a white house in the dunes, near the ocean. But Jack's mother is deaf to the sound of the waves, to the cries of the gulls and the children playing with their balls on the beach. She has drawn the white curtains in the kitchen as we speak to each other in short careful sentences, with guilty discretion. It's over a cold meal, a fish dish, an endive salad that we won't eat, our hands occasionally touching on the table in a gesture of impotent friendship. This house, this cottage, is where Jack grew up, and Jack's mother has no intention of leaving when winter arrives on the coast. The whole family used to get together here in the summer, she says in a toneless voice that will only come to life when Jack's name, Jackie, is mentioned. She raises a hand veined with blue blood to her forehead and asks me, lowering her eyes, how I met Jack. Was it at Harvard where he had a scholarship, or in Canada? I've already told her several times that it was in Cambridge on the banks of the Charles River, at Harvard, in the library, that I met Jack, but Harriet seems to have already forgotten. Oh, yes! she suddenly remembers, opening wide her grey-green eyes that are shining—Jack's eyes—Jackie told me that, wasn't it the day your bicycle was stolen and Jack lent you his, people loved my son for his grace, his elegant generosity, many people have praised those qualities in him. He was interested in German literature, he could recite Goethe, he'd begun to learn Italian, and I'd always encouraged him in those activities, I didn't want my son to be a typical American, we had such high hopes, he and I. Going to live abroad once his brothers had grown up.

All of them, one after the other, were called to serve their country. There was that horrible war, she sighs, brushing back a lock of hair, I couldn't wash my hair today, they forecast rain again; what are we going to do, she says in a voice clouded with grief and tears, how can we ever forget him? Steven and Eddie studied at MIT, they finished their studies after the Vietnam War, they're successful, I can't complain about them, they're good sons, they come to visit me here, Eddie would like me to move in with him, with his wife and children. But I'm happy here, in our home. I read a great deal, Jack's library is inexhaustible... What was he reading when you met him, Goethe, Dante? I tell her that Jack had abandoned his studies in literature by the time we met, that his concerns led him to the political works that had become almost obligatory reading in universities at the time. Harriet wasn't listening, she goes over to the refrigerator that is empty, she says, she's so sorry, she'd like to offer me dessert, but instead she'll give me a present, one of the books from Jack's library, a study of Dante she found in his jacket pocket, too bad the jacket had been dragged through the mud, his jeans and shoes were in such a state... before, she says, Jackie was always so well-dressed. But a student living on his own, without his mother, is often untidy, that was Jackie's downfall, finding himself alone so suddenly, on a university campus, without help, "struggling with...with...", but the demon will not be named, Jack's mother will retreat into a petrified silence. We move closer to each other sitting at the table, evoking first Jack's spirit, his courage when he became a conscientious objector, his dignity in prison, again his reading, Oriental thinkers towards the end of his life, and both of us will feel relieved, grateful to have preserved imperishable, the image of his body, although we are not always speaking of the same person; was his hair short or down to his shoulders? This image of Jack's young body, Jackie, is quickly blurred by the fear we both feel, Harriet and I, of seeing it wither in decay. The flower child, the hippie who preached free love, ecstasy through drugs, embraced his solitary death in an alleyway where his broken body would never stand again. When the time comes for me to leave, I ask Jack's mother if we can see each other again; she pushes me gently toward the door saying, "It's better for us to say good-bye, from now on I want to be alone in this house with Jack. You've probably already understood that... I stopped seeing people years ago."

## Notebook 30

*A leaden note* fills the air as we cross the threshold at Ruth and Gardner's house, a chromatic note that could rise from a Wagner opera, *Tannhauser*, perhaps, then a series of bristling, sumptuous sounds, it's Gardner's music when he composes at his piano in the music room. If it's cocktail time, we enter and leave the house to a clinking of glasses and voices as the sun sets over the water and Ruth and Gardner's grandchildren come running from the beach, exuberant, shaking their wet hair on the towels they wear around their necks. But whether it's evening or morning, Gardner is always at his piano on the top floor of the house overlooking the blue line of the horizon. Sometimes he listens to music by Ives, by Schoenberg, whose force and exaltation he admires, but his exploration of music is a determined quest for new sounds which can seem, to those of us who listen distractedly as we pass through his house, like an incomprehensible scramble of notes. Gardner used to be a concert pianist. Sometimes the aging musician, the composer with his birdlike head cocked over the abstraction of notes all day long, becomes that classical pianist again, Sundays, when he plays, with Mary standing beside the piano, on the flute, sonatas by Telemann and Mozart. From my studio in the pines, I listen to this melancholy Sunday music; occasionally

Gardner will interrupt a movement, saying to Mary: "Let's start over... this sonata is so light, so sweet to the ear...," and he sings as his fingers float over a beguiling ripple of notes.

When he returns to his own compositions, the lightheartedness of Mozart has disappeared, Gardner's fingers land furiously on a series of recalcitrant keys, the leaden notes are projected and expand, towards the bay, into the garden where Ruth tells her grandchildren: "Don't make any noise while your grandfather's working..." Ruth also tells her daughter, whose hand she is holding: "Your father is composing, he's writing an opera, he says, and he never shows his scores to anyone... Once again, this music will never be performed. It's too unusual. When will your father act like other people? All artists have to sell their work. We can't live off air and sound in this household..." Gardner eats very little, we never see him join his family for a meal. His kindness, however, draws all his grandchildren to his piano, sometimes he runs his fingertips over the downy heads of these babes. It's true, as Ruth says, that Gardner doesn't care about hearing his compositions performed. He says vaguely, "Some day, people will understand my music..." but the years go by and still no one has seen what he writes. Many years later, in Brittany, I'll begin a play, which Jean Faucher and Lucile Leduc will direct for television in Montreal, and in which Gardner becomes one of the characters: Jean, also a composer, a musician. While working on this text, *The Ocean*, which is first and foremost about writing, about a father who is a writer, about his influence on his wife and children and his spiritual legacy, Gardner's gentle face resurfaces, he will become Jean, the candid but stubborn musician, Gardner with his birdlike head.

In the play, as in real life with Gardner, music plays the role of softness, limpidity that contrasts so vividly with the harshness of writing and the writer. Ruth's words to her grandchildren are spoken by Judith, the musician's wife, to her children, "don't make any noise, your father is working." While a composer is working on Jean's music for the play, I hear in a café, while visiting San Francisco, a cascade of notes like a death knell, the notes of Gardner. Years later, his music is finally being performed, Gardner has agreed to share it; that incomprehensible chaos was us, our times.

# Notebook 31

*The hills of Wellfleet* and Truro, stripped by winter, still retain a few inhabitants; a few families isolated at the end of a row of pine trees, their houses nestled in marshes of snow-covered brambles, near the lakes; a few painters ravaged by solitude, and a few ghostly intellectuals who tread the pebbles of the shore during their morose strolls; but for all of them, Edmund continues to arouse their curiosity with an array of exotic characters who seem based on the puppets, sometimes kind sometimes evil, in his shadowpuppet plays. His agile fingers lift a corner of the black velvet curtain to reveal a puppet's foot still attached to the string, in its miniature silk boot, a prince, a witch, a demon with a hooked nose; tonight he amazes us all when he calls and says to Barbara, who never goes out in the evening: "Come over at six o'clock to meet Svetlana, Stalin's daughter, I think a great deal of her, a fascinating woman." The message is often that short and imperious, but it's an order.

In the biographies of Stalin we consult in Barbara's library, my eyes linger on two childhood photographs, one of Svetlana sitting beside her mother, a sombre madonna, an apparition of divine gentleness in this infernal household, whom Svetlana seems to adore, her head tilted to one side, grazing her mother's shoulder, and the other one, which I find more disturbing because the black velvet curtain parts to reveal a hellish scene, Svetlana, lolling, a chubby child in her beribboned dress, her thick stockings, her big shoes, Svetlana laughing at age ten in her father's arms. Her father who is Stalin. Barbara repeats that she won't be going out this evening, that she must finish her article for *Liberation* on the Peace March in Washington. Noble Paul and Nina from the now destroyed imperial Russia also shudder at the thought of such a meeting in the living room with the blue draperies, then Paul sighs in the hope of a reconciliation that seems inconceivable: "Stalin is the past, Nina, this poor woman is innocent, little Svetlana barely knew her mother who was assassinated under her father's dictatorship." Little Svetlana. It's around her, the little girl in the photograph sitting on the lap of a peasant, the son of a cobbler with a coarse jolly face, behind his bushy brown mustache, this good father and this good little girl who loves him, it's around them that we've gathered tonight: Elena scrutinizing her guest with her sharp, penetrating blue gaze, Barbara, shy but prepared to confront the calamities of the Stalinist era, the innumerable executions and bloody purges, Paul and Nina, condescending and reserved, in their shabby mended clothes, but it's better to get out, go to Elena's than to stay home in their cold house without a fireplace, says Nina, and besides they hope to hear this evening the rasping song of the Russian language, perhaps a poem by Pushkin, says Paul, which could sound so pure on the lips of Svetlana, who even as a young schoolgirl was enthralled by Pushkin's poetry. This passion for Russian literature, Svetlana tells us in a clear, detached voice, a detachment that chills me to the bone, this is what she's come to inculcate in American students, these barbarians in your wealthy universities, she says, along with the works of Kafka, that marvelous and implacable writer, but how can you understand Kafka in this country, she seems to say looking at us pointedly, accusingly. Edmund listens to Svetlana, the collar of his shirt open over his burgundy scarf. He'd so like Svetlana to feel comfortable in his house, he's even surrendered his own leather armchair where no one dares to sit, he asks Elena whether the shutters have been closed for there's a winter wind blowing, it's this wind and the racket of leaves flying against the window that is making Svetlana shiver under the woolen shawl she seems to have knitted herself since a few stitches are missing. "What a charming, cultivated woman," says Edmund to Paul who is listening to her attentively, "her book is soon to be published in New York and I'll mention it in one of my articles. Such heroic courage... I'm so glad she's decided to settle in our country with her husband. They're just back from India... that's where I met them at a conference... What a profoundly feminine woman..." "Ah, yes," says Paul, cocking his head, "such a courageous woman." These words are exchanged in the hallway while Elena, annoyed by the men's conversation, struggles to secure the shutters in the wind, then goes to the kitchen where her daughter Helen hands her a tray of hot drinks and cookies. Helen, who wants to go dancing at the discotheque with her teenage friends, the neighbours' twins whose hair falls to their waist like a golden shower, is begging her mother to let her go out. "No," says Elena strictly, "stay and listen to the grownups who have a lot to teach you." But Helen looks at the charming lady in the living room and doesn't want to know who Stalin was, let alone his daughter who, with her peachy complexion, her smile pasted on her plump face, looks as stiff as one of the teachers at her boarding school, the school near Boston where Helen is bored to death because she's always at the top of her class, in all her subjects. Meanwhile, Svetlana, calmer than when she arrived, touched by this welcome, speaks with renewed confidence about what she calls history's lesson; suddenly, she tells us frankly what we want to hear: the Soviet politicians who succeeded her father gave him an unjust reputation, he was once a pious man, a seminarian guided by his faith in God, he launched a political movement he believed to be salutary, but the revolution led him astray, he was blinded by glory. Doesn't anyone remember the books he wrote about the necessity of Marxism? Her father was the editor of a newspaper that improved the lot of his people, he survived several deportations to Siberia, he was a good father, he was my father, says Svetlana. And what about Trotsky? asks Barbara, interrogating Svetlana without anger, and Zinoviev and Kamenev, and many of his other disciples who were eliminated? So much torture, the concentration camps, the thousands of dead? What should we think about all that?, asks Barbara. "He was a good father," replies Svetlana in her placid voice, but when Nina asks what became of the dark madonna, Svetlana's young mother in the photograph, there's a long silence, then Svetlana replies in Russian to Paul and Nina, and for them alone, "Ah! Mama, mama who was so beautiful, they assassinated her…"

# Notebook 32

*O*n *these summer evenings* when the flames from the campfires on the beach rise against the deepening red of the sky, when the surf pounds the shore, all the couples are out on the beach, savouring the hot July air, and the clement breeze when night falls; everyone gathers, in the dunes and along the beach, dry pine branches that will crackle in the fire, and from shipwrecks, pieces of dark wood eroded by the tides, you can still see the round holes in the beams, the planks that have drifted in the water for years. The whole town seems to have gathered round these bonfires that reach for the sky, it's the celebration of sublime summers, even if the couples themselves, their faces purple in the fiery glow as they throw their twigs of wild roses and briars into the fire, continue to harass and torment each other. The wisest, the most dignified, the old philosophers, Adelaide and Charlie with their rosy cheeks beneath their straw hats, are sitting in their canvas deck chairs; their Celtic presence glows, a book on their lap, they quietly discuss the philosophy of Marcuse, or Reich, these are the philosophers of the day that Jack was reading at university. Adelaide remarks that "this industrial civilization is bound to end badly..." and Charles, this erudite man who writes books about the prodigious changes of the year 2000, replies, "After this industrial civilization will come the era of material wealth redistributed fairly among the nations. It will be paradise for our children, but we'll no longer be here." Gardner and Ruth are also there, in their chaise longues, exchanging similar thoughts with Adelaide and Charles, although Gardner, distracted, often stands up and wanders over to the water's edge, his feet in the surf, his white pants pulled up around his knees; he jots down a sound in his notebook, takes a recorder out of his pocket and plays some piercing Oriental, Japanese melodies, he'll explain later, which blend like echoes in the continuous cry of the gulls and the sound of the waves.

One of the children stops his race down the beach and reports breathlessly that his sandals were washed away in the waves; his parents pay no heed, that's Gilberte and Anthony telling Christopher to leave them alone, they have to talk. Christopher hears the shouts, the cries—will his parents finally separate this summer? "Unfaithful traitor, go ahead, take off and leave me with the kid, go live in New York with her... But you won't get away without leaving me everything." "That's not what I said," replies Anthony, his voice weakened by the blows he's received, because they've been quarrelling like this for days, in the woods, on the road, in Anthony's truck. "That's not what I want... I love my son, I can't live without him... He can come live with me in New York..." "Never, Christopher is mine! You'd have to kill me first, coward!" Forgetting about his lost sandals, Christopher sits cross-legged in the sand, he's whittling a boat out of a piece of driftwood with his jackknife; when the boat is finished, he'll fit it into a bottle, the captive boat will be part of his collection of figurative bottles, glass worlds in which pebbles, sequins of white sand float in sea water, along with the occasional goldfish, or a butterfly who will succumb after a few hours of this imprisonment, on the shelf of his dresser, in his bedroom. It's from the window of this room that Christopher contemplates his mother's haunted domain, her adjoining bedroom, and above it, the tower she's had built, from which she thinks she can hear, when she climbs up alone, the steps of German soldiers marching through the backyard. "What a mistake," says Gilberte, furious with her husband who's trying to untangle the string on a kite without looking at her, his yellow eyes beneath his scowling eyebrows staring at the blazing horizon, "what a mistake to have come to North America, out of love for you... I was crazy... I didn't know what I was doing. I was well-known in France, as a member of the resistance. After the war, I could have been given an official position like so many of my friends in politics. My God, what a mistake! Fortunately, Christopher came along..." "Christopher is part me, too" says Anthony, impassive, "I love the boy." "I hate you so much," says Gilberte. Around the dying embers, others laugh, dance, sing, cook fresh fish bought that afternoon at Wellfleet harbour, enjoying conversation and wine; I gather bits of wood to feed the fire; wearing red shorts on her long slim legs, Mary unfolds her canvas stool, a few feet from Christopher, close enough to do several sketches of Christopher's sulky profile, against the backdrop of the glowing red sky. I'm kneeling beside Robert and Jane who have turned to face the flames, the weather is warm, but for this outing which will be one of their last, Jane has wrapped herself up in a wool blanket, her hair once so thick and wavy, is growing back straight, bristly on top of her skull shaven for the treatments; Robert places his broad hands on Jane's skinny shoulders, he says to Charles and Adelaide, "As a militant black writer, I have to tell you my opinion has changed, I no longer believe in non-violence. The Black Panthers must take back our heritage, and that can't be achieved in this country except through armed violence..." "Really, my boy," says Charles, "what do you, who are so civilized, so intelligent, think you can possibly gain through terrorist means? Why don't you go live with Jane in Paris like James Baldwin... this country isn't ready for you yet... but wait a few years... it will be. Write... That's all you have to do, denounce us..." Robert stifles a sarcastic laugh. "Ah, write... write. Don't you realize that I can't any more... My publisher owes me a lot of money for my first book. And how can we leave when Jane is still sick..." "I'll get better," says Jane, pulling the wool blanket around her emaciated face, "besides, I've been feeling much better since the beginning of the summer... I'm in remission... I feel confident... right, Robert?" Robert is looking elsewhere, one of Charles' and Adelaide's daughters has joined us, she's a student in architecture at Harvard, she stretches languorously in her bathing suit on the sand, she finds Robert amusing, this young black man who has the fierceness of a lynx in his eyes, but she detects an enticing gentleness towards her, and increasingly, interracial relationships are accepted, as her father says, soon marriage between different races will be quite natural. Her father has always seen farther ahead than the others, like the philosopher Marcuse. Robert can read these thoughts in the young girl's amused, conciliatory expression. He leaves Jane, walks over to the student, "I don't agree with you about Marcuse... But we could discuss something else. Why don't you and your parents come for dinner at our house on Sunday..." "No, your wife isn't well enough," says the student, "I wouldn't want to disturb you..." The campfires crackle on the shore. We hear Jane's hollow voice say with the resignation of despair, "Do come for dinner on Sunday. I feel well enough... and it would make Robert so happy."

*hat is Barbara thinking* during these sweltering days in the month of August, aware as she is that her travels on this earth are coming to an end, that she is awaited far from the cheerful banks of the canal in Sugarloaf, far from these green waters where she loved to swim every day, and let herself drift in her rowboat? She can hear her friends laughing in the distance, in the trees with glossy leaves that rustle in the wind, they've picked the limes whose tartness is so thirst-quenching; from now on, she receives her friends in her house on piles, by the seashore, weak, she feels as if the little house could fly away with her, in the whirl of a cyclone, in a gust of wind from the dark suddenly overcast sky, towards the green waters of the canal, their furious overflowing carrying her to that other world which will soon be hers. The heat, the sun, the sweet warmth of the air that exhilarates her friends overwhelms her senses numbed by extreme fatigue, the cold penetrates her chest through the warm clothes she wears, a heavy fisherman's slicker, a plaid scarf, and on her feet, clumsy boots that protect her from the dampness and the constant sensation of cold that seems to follow her everywhere, the presence of death approaching, she thinks, remaining furtive, out of sight, yet nearby. She will never again return to the Far East, she won't travel across the country anymore, she'll never again see the walls of the Birmingham jail or her comrades Yvonne Klein, Ray Robinson fasting in their cells, those cells that were so close to hers she could send them messages through the bars.

She can see their emaciated faces turned to her behind the metal grating: "Take heart," says Yvonne, "take heart, just a few more days and the police will understand the goal of our non-violent action, we simply want to put an end to racism in this country." Barbara murmurs... "I'm so thirsty... It hurts more than all the harsh treatment. And you, Yvonne, so young and you look like a sick old lion..." Their coded messages on toilet paper, their conversations stolen from the silence of the walls are sometimes humorous: try to look cheerful and, whatever you do, don't give in to the guards when they tie your hands with ropes and try to force feed you.

But the thirst... to survive, they accept water. And the compassionate gesture of a guard who brings them a glass of orange juice—the miracle of quenched thirst. How Barbara, who can no longer feel, sense anything, except for the cold in her numb limbs, so close to uninterrupted sleep, her poor limbs gnawed at by sinuous pain, would love to experience, once again, the miracle of placing your lips on the glass, feeling the refreshing beads of moisture, the sharp taste of orange flowing down your throat. The young people under the trees savour the limes, their tart, bitter taste; what is the point of an entire life, so many battles and relentless struggles, thinks Barbara, if our existence is to end this way, in the passivity of crippled, aching limbs, numb to life's most delectable sensations?

And Louis, the cat, was bitten by a poisonous snake, this morning. Everything dies, perishes. Louis was buried under the oleanders, the gold-centered red hibiscus continue to bloom profusely this year. Leaning on her cane, Barbara gazes at the green waters of the canal, transparent in the light of the sun that warms them; soon her friends will bring out their canoes, their fishing boats, the children will go for a swim, in this profusion of lives that surround her, that of the dense, fragrant vegetation, the lives of the animals, the insects curled up in their secret hiding places in the sand beneath the plants. What is Barbara's life within the giant creation of nature that will go on living without her? She was no more than this butterfly with brown velvet wings that just came to rest on her hand. She came, she is leaving. But has the time come? Tonight or tomorrow?

No, not today. Some students from North Carolina are coming to meet her, to discuss her recent lecture at their university, just a few weeks ago, but the disease has undergone a sudden progression—so quickly, how to control the destruction now, the erosion in her muscles? That lecture spoke of the need to keep one's mind constantly free, "liberated;" moved by the power of her convictions, the students had promised to travel here to see her again, to show her what they'd written about her and the revolution of the sixties. Children, thinks Barbara, too young to have known those years of political upheaval.

But she would reveal this shameful past to them, the shame of Birmingham, the black people murdered in their schools and churches, perhaps these students from North Carolina would take up the battle. She felt so weary. Strangely, her thoughts kept straying to the tart taste of limes, how comforting it would have been to feel the sparkling liquid of limes flow down her throat, jolting ever so slightly the drowsiness of her body that had grown increasingly immobile, inert. She would have preferred not to see anyone today, to write a poem she could leave under the oleander bush, for Louis, to write as she did when she was fifteen, living in treehouses, scrambling over walls, when she was in a constant state of love for everything alive and quivering around her. Suddenly the wind was no longer stirring the leaves. It was undoubtedly time to meet the students who'd travelled so far to see her. When she went to her room that evening, she'd close the door carefully behind her, perhaps she'd have time to write a poem after all, with a bit more tenacity and perseverance, she might succeed.

In the poem she might write:

> I've turned off the lamp
> there is nothing but night
> I wait.

# Notebook 34

*ohn is in China,* says Barbara Hersey, I tell myself he's happy there, in the country where he was born and that one day, when he feels like it, he'll come back. That is how Barbara, the wife of the great writer John Hersey, in her wisdom, her deliberation, speaks to me several days after the ordeal of losing the man who had been not just a husband, but also a supportive loving friend during their long life together. Suddenly a magnificent couple is torn apart, one never knows who will disappear first, the man or the woman, says Barbara, but the first one to go leaves the other in such dreadful grief. We are sitting in the sun, Barbara and I, on the terrace at Café Exile where, just a few weeks ago, John was with us, beside his beloved wife and his friends, John Malcolm Brinnin, James Merrill, David Jackson. He was telling them about the novel he was writing, Asia still fascinated him; confident in the future, David told John that he'd still be with them for the publication of his complete works in September, the complete works of David, novels, essays, short stories and drawings he's finally accepted to publish at age seventy... "It's going to be a thick book," says David, "full of various things and will simply bear my name: David Jackson. Another title never occurred to me. Since this book is my entire life."

John Hersey was born the son of a pastor, in China. Several of his novels, his short stories take place in China or bear the mark of the Oriental impressions that were part of his childhood. John's mental balance, his philosophy of life, his self-effacement and his subtlety of mind are Chinese. It's painful to hear people talk about this energetic man in the past tense. In Cambridge, Jack and I used to read his books.

*Hiroshima*, John's most important testimony, moved us deeply. With the words of distress inspired by his compassion for the Japanese people, John accused the Americans, denounced the immensity of their crimes when they dropped, on August 6, 1945, the first atomic bomb that would claim more than 150,000 victims; so many of these victims would survive, alas, with their burned skin, their blind eyes, their limbs still maimed by fire like open wounds. At the time Jack and I were reading this book, Agent Orange was burning the rice paddies of Vietnam, generations of young Japanese were still perishing from the effects of the bomb that had obliterated the Japanese port. John Hersey went to Japan before writing his book, he had seen all the devastation he described. When we read his book, we knew that the great writer who taught literature at Yale University was overtly condemning the war in Vietnam and the perpetration of more massacres with napalm bombs.

I was among John's readers without knowing that I would meet him one day in Key West with Jim and David and our dear deceased publisher James Boatwright. The day would come when I'd see John's gentle face, his exaggeratedly tall body bending towards his friends, the head of a wise man, a slim head with dark eyes in which one could read the agility of his mind, the compassion of his heart as well. These qualities were immediately apparent in his gaze that lingered discreetly, trying to understand the other person, a humorous sizing-up. On a day when the radiant sun illuminates the entire island, so bright we can even see a black cat's tail in the shrubbery, the tail and its playful switching on the grass, I meet John on my bicycle and his silhouette seems to cast a sick shadow, a shadow heavy with sadness. John tells me he needs a lot of rest but he still writes every day, he talks about *Death of the Spider*, Neil Bishop's translation of Michèle Mailhot's novel (*La mort de l'araignée*) which he enjoyed immensely. John is interested in the problems of translation, it's something he often discusses with Richard Wilbur whose translations of Dante are well-known. On this particular day, although John is very worried about his own health, he is considerate enough to ask me if my work is going well, if the roof on the house has finally been repaired; I tell him that in this thankless winter of 1992, the catastrophes are neverending, I have to laugh as I show John my foot swollen from a scorpion bite. The weather is superb. John's shadow grows longer on the sidewalk. I can see his thin body, his tall shoulders bow under the weight of a burden he doesn't talk about.

On May 15, there will be a memorial celebration at Yale University in John's honour; Barbara, John's children, Brooke, John and Barbara's daughter, will all be there. "We'll be happy that day," says Barbara, "that's what John always expected of us, happiness. He had only a few hours left to live and he told us, whatever you do, don't cry, think of how happy we've been, and you must all go on being happy after I'm gone."

The white cottage under the palm tree, where friends gathered in the evening, the shed John had made into his study, where he liked to collect his thoughts every morning, Sam who barks the minute anyone crosses the threshold, the toy dog, a white ball with a black nose who can travel in a tiny basket, this is John's world, Barbara is still there to share it, but in the now acute silence of the man who left shrouded in his mystery. But the man who had the courage and the greatness to write *Hiroshima*, to empathize through the power of his words with the pain of 150,000 Japanese killed by the atomic bomb, with the incommensurable pain of an entire nation robbed, in several seconds, of their hopes, their future, robbed of several generations assassinated in their mothers' wombs; surely the man who wrote that book survives through his conscience, his mind that continue to influence us with pacific resonances.

John doesn't survive. He lives. He will always be alive. He is a historical witness and a prophet alarmed by the disasters of our time, famine and war. In his books, John tells us: "Hiroshima was yesterday, but Hiroshima could easily happen again today and this time there won't be any survivors."

# Notebook 35

*The wife of the famous poet and translator* enjoys going out alone. She sits straight on the seat of her bicycle, her cap pulled low over her eyes which she keeps shielded from our looks behind thick dark glasses. There was a time when everyone called them, her and her husband, the splendid couple, the golden couple. They are still, at over seventy, the flamboyant couple everyone notices when they stroll down the streets of the island in the evening, hand in hand, in their white suits, their bare feet in leather sandals. They are taller than everyone, their posture is proud and dignified, when they return from the sauna, from the palm grove where they play tennis, an aura of magic surrounds them, they love each other, they are beautiful, this magical aura that illuminates their faces without wrinkling them, the air they breathe seems to come to them from the land of immortality. And yet, they know they, too, are going to die. They say so: "We'll arrange things so it ends without ugliness, without decay." If one tries to get to know them better, they withdraw proudly, keep their distance, their complexity makes them impenetrable. A photograph taken in the sixties, in the company of the writer Lillian Hellman, their friend, reveals the glowing beauty of their youth. It's amazing to see how little they've changed. But the poet's wife, so talented, was writing then, and today she no longer writes. She enjoys going out alone, without friends, without witnesses. When I meet her at Patrick's bar, Square One, she doesn't see me, behind her dark glasses, she sips a martini, exchanging a few words with Patrick, making sure that he alone can hear. But I overhear these words: "It's important not to be weak," she says, "you should never let others see your weaknesses..." "It's true," says Patrick tenderly, "but I'm sorry to learn that you hurt your hip when you fell. Does your husband know?" "Oh no, he mustn't find out," says the poet's wife, in her inexorable pride.

She is standing, her elbows on the bar, straight and inaccessible; there were so many years of glory, for her and him, so much success; her husband is leaving for Sweden where he'll receive still another literary prize, she'll accompany him, and once again as in the past they shall be the golden couple. But she won't mention her hip accident to her husband, she doesn't want to disappoint him, she won't be that imperfect. She intends to say nothing.

I often meet her like this, she who enjoys going out alone and, leaving her to her invisibility, I don't talk to her. But at the island library, I read the books she wrote, beautiful collections of poems published in the sixties. Like the works of Mary McCarthy and Robert Lowell, they are the works of a politically committed writer. I wonder why these poems received so little attention from American critics, in the *New York Review of Books*. The wife of the famous poet attends painting exhibitions alone, I learn from her books that she paints and that she has exhibited in galleries in New York, in Boston. That was in the sixties.

One day, my footsteps follow hers all the way to Bahama Village where she strolls alone in the noonday sun, heading directly for a street she seems to know well. She starts chatting amiably with a black man, standing on his veranda. "Right here, next to your house," she says, "is where we're going to build a museum for black painting. We'll show only black painters." The man listens to her, they talk at length. "I've already met with several painters from Bahama Village... this town has ignored you for too long... So much wasted talent..."

"Come in," says the man, "I have some paintings to show you." But that particular evening, the evening of her hip accident, as she sips her martini standing at the bar, inviting Patrick alone into her precious isolation, the features of her face look drawn behind her thick dark glasses, worry suddenly mars the harmony of her face. Once again the wife of the poet confides in Patrick: "Is it possible that we're all so fragile? I don't want to be ill, ever... I still have so many projects... very personal projects... Don't we all have a secret life that must be protected, sometimes even from those we love most?" This other life, these projects are her visits with her friends in Bahama Village, the museum of black painters, and, the writing she tackles alone. This return to writing is slow and difficult; after several martinis, the wife of the poet removes a notebook and a pen from the belt she wears around her waist when riding her bicycle; she looks pointedly away from us all, behind her dark glasses, and she begins to write. "These will be my memoirs, from the splendid, crazy years," she says with a smile to Patrick, "but I'll never publish them." For why write, she thinks—aren't my thoughts too distracted, too frivolous? She remembers bitterly her early works, so unappreciated, read by no one, her soul sleeping on dusty library shelves, and her smile freezes. Late that evening, Patrick will find crumpled, torn pieces of paper, pages torn out of the notebook containing a few illegible signs, but one title written in blue ink on a blank page: "The Story of a Woman."

And gradually, the wife of the poet will return less frequently to write in the bar, she'll travel for a long time in Sweden with her husband; when I finally see her again, strolling elegantly in the streets of Bahama Village, searching for another breath of fresh air among the black painters, as usual, she won't notice me, she who enjoys going out alone, she who has, far from her husband, another life...

# Notebook 36

*There's a bronze sculpture* in a garden in France. A portrait of Paul, our friend Paul Sablon, in a garden near Chartres, a sculpture with a history. When the person who is sculpting it has finished and polished it, it will reflect the light of the summer skies; its stark angles, when night falls, will receive the rains and the first blasts of cold. This is how Paul will go on living among us. He who expresses in his impeccable French, his love of the seventies, "what sexual liberation, in those days, have we ever before known such freedom in our lives on this earth, and we were the ones, the people of my generation, who decided it should be so...", he tells me, his eyes shining; Paul, this luminous eccentric from Scandinavia, is sharing a noontime beer with me, before returning to his construction work, for he is building his own house—which will let in the rain whenever it pours on the island. This infatuation with the seventies, the freedom and imagination of those years, he still exudes it during our brief conversations on his terrace in bloom, in a neglected yard where hens peck at the sun-scorched grass; there's Paul in these moments of relaxation, of leisure, almost nude in his cut-off shorts, an earring in his right ear, another one, as narrow as a wedding band, through the tip of his left nipple, his hair blond as straw closely cropped; he sparkles with ardour, with intelligence, and he is passionate about culture, he reads Jean Genet, the German philosophers whose works he pores over in German, "you have to read everything," he says with his whimsical exuberance, "and study everything too... work on a Ph.D.in art history, even if it's a bit late..."

He will read all those books, he will receive his diploma in art history, his curiosity is boundless, he has to keep moving, traveling, his wandering is stylized and scholarly, from the museums in France to the museums of Holland, spending time in the summer in the forests of Norway; his family ancestors were, he tells me, pastors, religious philosophers who wrote theological works, his princely nostalgia occasionally soars to these pure regions of Northern Europe where he hopes to settle some day with his wife Pamela. But it's in France, in the peaceful countryside near Chartres, that he most enjoys living, growing his flowers. Pamela, Paul. Seductive to the extreme, with the romantic androgyny they perfect in their fanciful art of dressing, of living; they are, in fact, from a singular Europe whose decadence is not decrepitude but the charm of novelty, of subtle provocation. They enjoy celebrating Scandinavian Easter with vodka and smoked salmon; they entertain—in their home in Key West with its walls that collapse before they're built letting in the torrential rains that stain their expensive clothes—counts and marquises, on their balconies where, among their cats, thread-bare bathing suits hang to dry, they entertain anyone who will bring news from afar—the male prostitute from Milan or the bankrupt millionaire who wanders barefoot through their living room, anything outside the cult of the imagination bores them. Together they follow their flamboyant path like shooting stars, they are dual, both man and woman, girl and boy, perhaps they are two seraphim stranded on Earth, casting in their scintillating wake the rays of their twinned blonde heads.

In his overgrown garden in Key West, Art Kara welds together pieces of bronze, the rough version of the sculpture already suggests the final form, thinks Art; can't we recognize the movement of Paul's body, his graceful gait along the fence on Griffin Lane; if the head is tilted, it's because Paul would often freeze in this reflective pose, withdrawing suddenly into this stern profile, that of one of his ancestors who had studied the depths of the soul. For Paul was all this, chaos and rigour at once. And Art is cleaning the sculpture, placing it back on its pedestal. "Do you remember," he asks David and me, "how he'd flex his knees while walking..." "A trace of the child in him," says David, "God, how I loved his craziness, we'll never meet anyone like him again." "The real sculpture, the one I'll sculpt for Pamela, outside her house in France, will be the same size as Paul," says Art, "he was built like one of those long Giacometti sculptures... his head often bowed solemnly. It's the position of his head that's given me the most trouble. It makes you think he'd known for years what was in store for him... charming and entertaining us all the while. He cast the spell of euphoria, the intoxication of all pleasures, and yet what a serious, profound boy."

There's a bronze sculpture in a garden in France. There's the abandoned house in Key West that I'll leave in March 1992. Paul came there alone in my absence to plant new spring flowers, he covered his bed, he who is so joyful, with Mexican funeral hangings, then he left for New York to receive his university diploma. When I see him again in this garden in

France, the light on his face is intense, not a single wrinkle has creased it, humiliating pain has not yet marred it in the hospital near Chartres. When winter arrives with its cold winds, the resistant material of bronze will ward them off, a light snow will fall on Paul's broken neck, on his head bowed forever.

# Notebook 37

*rom behind the curtains* and shutters of their Wellfleet houses comes the muffled murmur of calumny, of vilification, everyone is tattling, gossiping, because Robert, the black man this fine community of intellectuals, of artists, had finally accepted—"tolerated," says Gilberte to her neighbours, "since when do we need to socialize with a black delinquent who doesn't work and is supported by a white woman, when the poor woman is on her death bed,"—the one everyone now considers "just another black man" who squandered his promising début as a writer, praised by New York critics, has a relationship with a young white girl, Christine, the daughter of Charles, the philosophy professor. And what a disgrace, says Gilberte, Charles and Adelaide don't blame Robert, they welcome him into their home, discussing with him as they always did Wilhelm Reich, and the revision of the role of sexuality in modern psychoanalysis. People say these conversations last late into the night, that from the beach one can see through the window, by the light of the moon, the gesticulating silhouette of Robert who gets carried away defending fake theories, because, says Gilberte, "what can this uneducated man from Harlem possibly know about Wilhelm Reich?" Gilberte tells anyone who will listen, on the phone, in the street when she walks home from the post office to the woods where she lives in isolation with her son—all because of her husband who left her for a younger woman, she claims—Gilberte insists that she is not a racist, she admits she often desired Robert, no, she is not a racist, she is humiliated, as is Jane, by Robert, as are, she says, all women by the men who betray them bold-facedly, hence the need to defame, to destroy Robert, to repudiate him, ban him from our homes, our towns. This vicious mood that Gilberte hisses into our midst between her bared teeth and the despair of a rejected woman don't seem to affect Robert who, at sunset, embraces Christine in the dunes, as they roll together in the warm ripples of sand, oblivious to the sharp grasses and flowers that grow there; they are free, exercising their agile limbs, singing, dancing on the sand baked by the August sun, they run in a single leap between the sun and the sea, far from the cruel gossip, the murmur of hate. "I saw them," says Gilberte, "at the campfires those nights in July... embracing in the firelight shamelessly, almost in full view of Jane who hid her face with her shawl."

In fact, far from hiding her face, Jane sees everything and no trace of blaming Robert can be detected in her feverish eyes. To the few visitors she still receives at her bedside she says, frail and unsteady in her white house where the shutters will soon seal her mute bedroom: "I encouraged Robert to withdraw from me, he accompanied me for so long throughout the treatments at the hospital. The rest is nothing but scandal... I don't want him to see me suffer, I love him too much for that. I simply hope he doesn't have any children with Christine, it would be a terrible pity for an innocent child to be maimed by our prejudice, our racism. Neither Robert nor Christine could survive that."

During this relationship which will be short—for Christine who is eighteen will soon love other boys when she returns to Harvard in September, but nine months later she'll come back to Robert with a mulatto child who'll have Robert's striking beauty—during this short summer of sensual happiness, Robert will write and write, putting aside his autobiography for essays on the future predicted by an Austrian psychiatrist who addresses primarily the white middle class whose minds he hopes to refine with his vision of the progress of industrial civilization, a future Robert will describe in a sarcastic prophecy for the forgotten men, and the women who also go unmentioned in this civilization, the men and women of the black race.

But they too will bear the brunt of his caustic thoughts, of his lucid judgement, even if this time Charles, the professor, doesn't approve of the cynical aspect of Robert's insights. Robert predicts that the just and violent incantation of the Black Panthers will finally cease to be heard, that these rebels will be replaced by comfortable men and women. Robert imagines—he could have written some of today's television series —black people parading on television as Whites for whom they'll become models in comforting, reassuring sitcoms where, as if in a poisonous ether, the real problems of the Blacks will disappear, will be denied in favour of a demeaning blandness that finds its source in white materialism. Suddenly African Americans will no longer have a history, a past. The spectre of slavery will be erased. We'll watch a good black father come home from work at night to confront his children's rebellions and lies, no different from those of white children, and armed with the same virtuous advice, the black father like the white father will tell his boys:

"Don't take drugs," and his daughters, "Don't stay out late at night, remain virgins until the day of your marriage." Thus the white decay will gradually contaminate the purity of black blood, writes Robert. And Charles, reading these pages in his chaise longue on the beach, will say to Robert, with gestures of protest toward Christine and Robert sitting at his feet: "But, Robert, why write this outrageous book? We will never forget what the people of Africa have suffered because of us. And they will never forget what we did to them. There will never be such a thing as a comfortable black man. You are a perfect example, Robert, you who are always so dissatisfied and unhappy."

Staring at the horizon, Robert will slip his arm around Christine's waist and reply: "Yet it's true, Professor, it will happen, in your fantasy of comfort my brothers will forget everything, they will be anaesthetized and they will die of the same evils as you."

# Notebook 38

*He is a young man* who lives alone, on a wooded hill. He lives a few paces from the house Barbara has lent me so I can write during this lush spring on Pamet Point Road where, along the paths leading down to the woodsy hollow of Paradise Valley, the scent of wild roses fills the air and swallows flit around their nests, in terror of the predatory blue jays. The young man rarely leaves his house with the weatherbeaten grey shingles. Gilberte says he's just come back from Hollywood and that he enjoys this solitary existence, "who knows, maybe he's unhappy," she says in the hope of someday visiting this laconic and mysterious solitude, but the young man is unsociable and hostile to any overtures. When I write or sketch outside, with my faithful Gilou wagging her tail around me, her paws scratching the ground, her nose relishing the fresh smell of the grass still damp with frost, (Gilou the Labrador is only two years old and it's her first season of freedom since we adopted her at the SPCA in Provincetown), when spring is so sparkling that everyone is outside, in their yards, on the beaches, along the roads on their bicycles, the young man doesn't come out because he's learning his lines. In the summer, I catch a glimpse of him through the sunny gap in the cedar hedge, on his hill—so thin in his white chinos, he's carrying a canoe on his shoulders, a fishing canoe that he ties to the roof of his jeep. Suddenly he turns his head and sees me, his shy smile lasts but an instant, but I see the dimples in his cheeks, his brown hair is cut very short, shaven with precision over his ears, a lock of straight hair falls over his forehead, he brushes it back with his hand. "A real little boy or a doe fleeing a hunter," says Gilberte, "an adorable boy if he weren't so determined to live alone." Already the brief apparition can no longer be seen through the green splashes of cedar in the sunlight. Inside the house with the grey shingles, the young man is reciting his lines.

In the town of Wellfleet, his name is often murmured, whispered, isn't he the boy who played the main role in the pacifist play *Beach*, in the days of the cold war between nations? He was also seen in the demonic role of Bates, the awkward killer in *Psycho*, one remembers his twisted smile in the classic by Hitchcock, but the young man who lives alone in the woods seems to have been overwhelmed by the roles of murderers in horror movies; like his father, Osgood Perkins, who was a stage director before turning to film, he is first and foremost an actor who understands the subtleties of his profession, a studious and committed artist. Very young, in 1956, he received a first Oscar nomination for his part in the film *Friendly Persuasion*. Ever since the blare of publicity surrounding *Psycho*, the young man has lived in hiding, sometimes, but very seldom, entertaining actor or director friends who come from New York and Los Angeles. That is how an astonishing lady named Michaela happens to knock at the door of the yellow house—she reminds me of Frances with her stature and her broad sculptor's hands—she is a close friend of the young man who lives in his retreat. She abruptly asks me whether I write for the theatre and together we read

*The Execution* written for Yvette Brind'Amour who will direct it at Montreal's Théâtre du Rideau Vert; Michaela would like to see the play translated into English, she'll begin a meticulous translation, on the very day of our first meeting which will also be our last, for she lives in Los Angeles; later the play will be translated by the marvellous David Lobdell who will translate so many works from Québec with the same concern for truth and poetic elevation, a translator who was also a poet and a novelist and whose presence among us is sorely missed today.

Michaela who, like Frances, has the eye of a painter, a blue-grey gaze quick to perceive, has noticed the unusual colour of the walls and the floors of the house where I'm staying and says: "Those are the colours of the painter Emil Nolde, aren't they?" It's true, Barbara, with her usual tolerance, having allowed me to repaint the cottage in keeping with my penchant for warm, sunny colours, the yellow house has become one of Nolde's landscapes, a landscape discovered in one of the painter's travel diaries forgotten in a collection of foreign books, in this diary published in Munich under the title *Südsee-Skizzen*, the painter returns to these colours: azure blue for the sky, the sun setting over the tropical sea is bright orange dipped in red, and the yellow house so securely anchored to these piney hills, like the house of the secretive young man, sets sail in a swell of colours toward the distant south seas. The walls are an opaque blue, the floors yellow and orange like Nolde's sun; with an approving nod, Michaela says she loves these walls and as she leaves me with a handshake, she pronounces the young man's name, "Anthony, Tony, who's so sensitive."

I'll never catch another glimpse of the solitary young man through the sunlit opening in the cedars, that summer on Pamet Point Road, but on September 19, 1992, I'll imagine him in his true grandeur when he reads his last words a few days before his death at age sixty in his house in Hollywood, when he tells a journalist, surrounded by his wife and sons: "Many people believe that AIDS has been sent to this Earth as a curse, as God's revenge. I don't believe that, but I think that if so many are suffering from this disease on this Earth, it's so we can learn the true meaning of love and comprehension, of tenderness and compassion. I learned more about love and charity in a few months spent with those stricken with AIDS than in all my years in the competitive, fierce world of theatre and film where everyone is slitting everyone else's throat, where there is no place for an ageing actor. Without this disease, I never would have understood that love exists..."

These words, were they not what he was saying in the silence of his house on the hill? "We don't know how to love, that's why I never go out," he seemed to say to those who saw nothing more in him than a brilliant actor overwhelmed by his fame, when in fact, he was already fleeing that which had always frightened him, the darkness of this world.

## Notebook 39

*O*n *April 30, 1970,* President Nixon announces his decision to prolong the war by sending American troops to invade Cambodia. On all the university campuses, the students the president calls "hoodlums," in his lack of respect for their youthful idealism, the students all across America revolt. May 4th is a cool spring day in the hills and mountains that surround Kent State University—the scene of a vast student demonstration for peace. On that day innocent people will die in the crowd, in the midst of their grief-stricken comrades, killed by soldiers from Ohio's National Guard, they'll fall victims to rifles and gunshots a few feet from their murderers, between a classroom, Taylor Hall, and the pagoda which was probably a temple for meditation; it has been clearly established through film footage, and the testimony of photographers, that William Schroeder, Sandra Scheuer, Jeffrey Miller, Alison Krause were executed in cold blood by the army on May 4, 1970, on that spring day in the hills of the university campus.

In American households, there's an uproar of protest: "They killed our children, they killed our children! Our innocent children!" All the parents who watch the horrible massacre on television the evening of May 4th, see their own child's death in the distorted features of William, Sandra, Jeffrey, Alison, lying on the lawn or spilling their blood on the asphalt of the street where the demonstrators and spectators of these crimes rush by, waving their black flags. Gilberte says to Anthony: "That boy they shot twice could be Christopher." Elena thinks of her daughter Helen who is now at university, everyone fears for their children, their lives, these same parents cry when they watch the events of this day of mourning replayed with atrocious precision: unarmed, their hair in the wind, the students advance towards the formidable army chanting, "Make love not war, we want flowers not bombs." The soldiers from the National Guard attack them with a blast of chemical clouds (tear gas which, according to army officials, is inoffensive, causing nothing but tears) creating a fog, a barrier of smoke around the wounded and blinded demonstrators, suddenly cornered from all sides by a hypocritical army of hateful soldiers commanded by a general in civilian clothes.

The students who calmly assembled at noon, these hippies from good families, with their beards, their plaid shirts, who dream of life and love in the country, these children of alienation, the brothers and sisters of my friend Jack disperse now in terror, shouting and calling for each other in desperate voices, "Jeffrey, where are you?" "Alison!" These scenes on a battlefield of springtime green, between a classroom and a meditation place, in the midst of flowers still budding, these scenes of affliction, this is what American parents will see on the evening of May 4th, in front of a cheery fire, or over the family's evening meal, and everyone will see his daughter or her son, their own children led to death, shot in the back, caught in the gunfire. And these really are their children, the ones they wait for at home in the evening, or expect soon, for summer vacation, the plans are already made, these are the children of prosperous white middle-class America, the children who leave deep wounds when they disappear. These same parents felt great compassion when they saw—on this same family television screen—the black students killed in a demonstration in Alabama, they were frightened, appalled by the state of the world, but never did they think that their own children could die in this same war, this now total war, without regard for race or class, this war that, indirectly, they had provoked themselves.

For, secretly, hadn't they approved of police violence to teach these dissatisfied young people who were always criticizing their elders a lesson? Weren't they forced to admit they didn't like this ideology of peace?

And now before them are the faces, in graduation photographs, the glowing faces with sparkling white teeth of William Schroeder, of Sandra Scheuer, and Jeffrey Miller whose death was long and painful with his classmates crouched over him trying to resuscitate him, his blood flowing from his skull, from his lacerated temples; Alison Krause, beautiful and idealistic; Joseph Lewis who was shot twice; these children of ordinary Americans are vigorous, bursting with health, perhaps each one is also a model student, destined for a brilliant future; the future they had imagined with emotion and fervour when listening to the words of the Kennedy brothers, Martin Luther King, Malcolm X.

In his book *The Truth about Kent State*, published in 1971, writer Peter Davies appeals to American justice to undertake a new investigation of this tragedy that casts such shame on the collective conscience of a nation—under the Nixon administration, the appeal for an investigation is rejected by the Attorney General. Various religious associations, including the United Methodist Church, support the author's demand and are determined to find those guilty of these murders; the murderers will appear to be good citizens simply doing their duty, or so they claim, sergeants or officers, who only acted with such murderous violence in self-defense, because the students, "those hoodlums," were throwing rocks or bricks at them, some of them can even prove how viciously they were attacked or provoked by the students. They simply did their duty—what choice did they have?

On May 4, 1970, students like Jack, others who could have been my friends' sons or daughters, beautiful children, enjoying the breeze in their hair, inhaling the mild spring air, march, their books under their arms, toward their assassins who are masked in steel, armed with guns, with bombs, and they chant, "Flowers not death..."

# Notebook 40

*I*t's hunting season on the Cape Cod peninsula. In the woods, the rusty forests which will soon turn dark brown before the first snowfall, hare and pheasants scurry anxiously toward the safety of their hollows. In her car driving along the ponds, the uniform expanse of fields still rosy at five o'clock in the afternoon, the cranberry bogs with their vivid hues, Elena is shivering despite her blue sweater, thinking that she has undoubtedly gone for her last swim of the year in the icy ocean; she, whose physical fitness has always been unshakable and haughty, doesn't like feeling this sudden susceptibility to the cold, and even less hearing the thin cough rattling in her chest.

She'll call Nina as soon as she arrives home, it will be comforting to invite her for a chat beside the fireplace in the big empty living room. But Paul and Nina are dead, their backs became stooped, like her own once so straight back, she thinks, bowed over the parched crevices of the earth in autumn. But every evening, around this time, she thinks, "I'll call Nina...and Paul, they'll come for tea..." and abruptly she remembers that, like her husband, they are no longer with her, or still so close she can feel their faint presence in the cedar-shingled house; when five o'clock, six o'clock chimes on the old grandfather clock, in the big living room, she'll realize that there is no longer anyone at her side, not even Old Boy, the dog who just yesterday was snoring in his sleep in the spacious leather armchair. She'll continue to read the books, which are still there on the marble table, next to the fireplace, she'll read some passages from these books by Teilhard de Chardin, Simone Weil, from which, not so long ago, she prepared with concise notes, Edmund's reading programme, but she'll be easily distracted, unmotivated, removing her glasses, putting them back on, staring at the flames on the hearth.

Elena can hear her own footsteps as she enters the deserted house, steps that sound heavy, slightly shuffling; with a long-stemmed match she re-ignites the fire under the pine kindling—will she finally be rid of this bronchitis, this cough when her daughter comes to visit at Easter? Will she be able to wait that long, this solitude in the house that just yesterday was always full is such a new and disconcerting sensation. Perhaps, but, she thinks, if her faith in God were stronger, wouldn't she be more courageous in facing sickness and old age, something her friends Paul and Nina accomplished in silence and with stubborn dignity? Where are the poets, where is the writer, Waldo Frank, who so often came to chat with her in the evening, where is Dickinson, the subtle painter of the Truro marshes? She feels a pang of nostalgia; perhaps her friends no longer go out, fleeing the cold and the wind off the sea, in their cottages in the dunes.

She walks into the kitchen still bathed in sunlight at this time of day; standing in front of the photograph over the counter of the smiling Kennedy family gathered on the beach in

Hyannis Port, she pours, but this time only for herself, the ritual six o'clock whiskey, over ice cubes that rattle dully in the glass; her fingers still feel stiff from the cold as she rubs her hands together. In their red rubberized armour, their padded raincoats, the hunters comb the woods, the fields, the pine groves, their rifles raised in front of them. Elena can see them from the window, in the orchard where Helen took her first steps, a tiny child bringing an apple to her parents with a willful look that already revealed her strong-minded character, they are trampling on the delicate nests, the clumps of earth and grass of the rabbits' and birds' shelters. That is how she surprised them this afternoon in her car, these hunters who come to kill the deer in the woods, whose threatening cries drown the sleep of the sandy land in winter.

This hostile chorus of hunters that disturbs her quietude mingles in her memory with the shouts and cries of hunters chasing deer with their dogs, in the forests of Europe. The herds of deer flee, in the woods, the forests, they're surrounded by the hounds: sometimes a majestic stag stops in a clearing, wounded, he no longer follows the others; his ears perked, he listens, the softness of the autumn sky flows in his gaze. Suddenly he resumes his flight through the leaves, exhausted, but the hunters, sadistic, refusing to let him escape, pursue him beyond his territory. They make him lose his way, frighten him and the dying stag is shot down on the railroad tracks.

In the solitude of her empty, cold house, separated from her loved ones, Elena reflects that those forests of Europe have followed her in her exile, in her departures from country to country, that these cries of triumphant hunters will never fall silent. Men are capable of the most vile acts, she thinks. Who will help them rise above such baseness?

Then as the heat slowly warms her limbs, she forgets the funereal voices. Once again she sees her daughter Helen walking toward her under the apple tree, she is delighted to have such a strong-minded daughter, a child who showed determination in her very first steps, in the summer grass, who walked toward her, imperturbable, to place an apple in her lap. A child who, like her, will have the strength to survive all the tribulations on this earth. She muses that she is suddenly very alone in the house with the blue draperies, but such is her fate, Elena will possess till the end the simplicity of being happy, and tomorrow, if it's a bit warmer than today, she will once again brave the harsh waves of the wintry ocean.

# Notebook 41

*T*he *New York critics* describe him as the grandson of Henry James, of Marcel Proust; when he publishes his book *Sextet*, with his studies of the works of T.S. Eliot, Alice B. Toklas, Elizabeth Bowen, Henri Cartier-Bresson, Edith Sitwell, he is already a poet, critic, biographer, historian, he is also the man of everlasting friendships—John Malcolm Brinnin, whose literary analysis goes beyond documented research on the work and penetrates the heart of the writer, his or her character, often capturing the mystery of the artist's lost innocence.

And so that's how, in the evening on the beach, near the rocks where the waves are crashing violently, he speaks like a friend, a brother, of Dylan Thomas, and his martyred fate, of Truman Capote, this particularly beloved friend for whom he will write, two years after Truman's death, the tender portrait, *Truman Capote, Dear Heart, Old Buddy*, (a title I've always found impossible to translate into French since the "dear heart" and "old buddy" express an almost metaphysical fraternal bond between the two writers). Eight years older than Truman Capote, John Malcolm is also his guardian, the sensible protector who dares criticize his friend's unruly behaviour and tries to prevent him from erring when blinded by flamboyant success.

Standing in front of a window blind, his eyes half-closed over an elusive smile, Truman Capote is still a boy, a brilliant adolescent when Rollie McKenna takes his photograph in the forties; when John Malcolm meets him at Yaddo, the artists' residence in upstate New York, he is seduced by the ingenuousness of the young man with the round cheeks, and by his extraordinary precociousness; Truman Capote is already the unexpected prodigy, the gifted child of American letters, and John Malcolm, fearing that fame will go to this juvenile head too fast, watches over him with the sternness of an angel.

The course of John Malcolm's reminiscences over the years, whether he shares them in person or in writing, takes us into the life of the younger writer, into the changing landscapes of his existence, as if we had always been part of that life, following the inner doubts, at the time of the publication of his first books, the books the critics greet with initial indifference; up to the mysterious acclaim of *In Cold Blood* when the author, weakened by such sudden monstrous success, will succumb to his penchant for socializing and will be slowly destroyed, as will some time later my friend, Robert, by the arrogant society which at first scorned his genius.

John Malcolm is sensitive to these transformations, both physical and moral, in his friend always on the run, constantly seeking a peaceful place to write, think, reflect, before the frivolity of high society catches up with him again, before he is consumed by drugs and alcohol, before the purity of the blond boy, who is still so childish and playful at John Malcolm's side in Venice, is completely tarnished. Young Truman, the hypochondriac, tells his friends he has leukemia, but his travels lead him to North Africa—and suddenly there's a photograph of him in a chateau in Switzerland, holding a dog in his arms. What will become of him?, John Malcolm asks himself, when will he stop succumbing to these vain attractions that interfere with his writing?

But the same unbridled Truman writes to his friend John Malcolm, urging him not to be discouraged by his erratic behaviour, he is first and foremost a writer, something his detractors do not understand, the originality, the depth of his talent are misunderstood, "the man who makes the bees dance," as John Malcolm says when reciting his poems at the Poetry Center in New York, the man whose words sing among the flowers, like the sentences of Jean Genet, the illuminated Truman, writes that he is beginning a novel, a novel inspired by a macabre incident reported in a Kansas newspaper; this novel will surpass the tone of fiction, it will be a Dostoevsky novel of modern times, a work of brutal realism, merciless for both the executioner and the victim— it will be the novel *In Cold Blood* which will bring its author wealth but also great uneasiness, dissatisfaction.

It is this dissatisfied, unhappy friend, still the same dissipated child, who comes to see John Malcolm in Key West; the child is now a rich man John Malcolm finds unlikable. He drinks to excess, John Malcolm speaks to Truman gently, reminding him again that writing is what matters most to him. It's a grey day in October during the rainy season in Key West, in the sixties, the island is poor, deserted, lacking in comfort: John

Malcolm tells Truman he intends to live here, in geographic isolation, that he has chosen this solitude. Truman takes a cheque book out of his pocket, saying he can buy a house wherever he wants, he offers a real estate agent a cheque for 10,000 dollars; John Malcolm observes his friend corrupted by money but doesn't judge him—such chagrin, such pain and disappointment, he thinks, to have transformed his friend in so little time. Yet behind the sarcastic, sometimes callous laugh, he thinks he can hear the voice of the young Truman who once wrote to him: "Baby Angel, help me." The *enfant terrible*, the Radiguet of American letters has preserved his childish purity and his impudent smile, but suddenly, so quickly, like the Radiguet of *Diable au corps*, there is no longer a trace of his effulgent life.

# Notebook 42

*It's during this summer of blazing light* on the beaches of Truro when the August sun shines on the waves of the ocean until even the waters are warm, it's during this summer of race riots in the streets of New York, of Harlem, that Robert's and Christine's son is born. Gilberte, who seems to regret her harsh attitude toward Robert, says that "only this child can save Robert, rehabilitate him in the eyes of others, make him into a responsible man..." Robert hears the dull drone of this backbiting all around him, these ceaseless voices persecuting him: one can only hope, say the voices, that the couple's child will look more like his mother, that his hair will be blond like Christine's, that he'll have blue eyes, white skin. But when Jonathan is born, Christine's parents are quick to remove him from the sight of his enemies, no one sees the child during the first months of his life; Christine's parents, Robert, Christine and the child stay hidden in one of Anthony's cottages high on the hill. Anthony alone knows the secret of this isolated place where he sometimes retires to live on his own, far from his marital hell; he used to bring his son Christopher here, to go fishing with him on the silent lake, but Anthony's precious child grew up so quickly, the cottage on the hill is empty now, and Anthony drifts on his raft in solitude. It's while drifting like this on the shimmering water of the lake, one evening, that he imagines how safe the black child could be here, in this refuge, far from the meanness of the village. That's where the mysterious babe in arms is taken, where his mother nurses him; he's a joyous, robust baby who makes Robert very proud, he envelops the mother and child in his adoring gaze; when Jonathan is six months old, the three of them will go to live in Paris where Robert will see his books published in French, this vision of a better future, Robert shares it with Christine's father, Charles, the elderly philosophy professor. They'll leave, he says, they'll be free, they will have deserved their hard-won right to freedom and happiness; but as he speaks with such easy eloquence, Robert doesn't seem to notice the distressed look in Christine's eyes as she rocks the child; nor do Christine's father and mother seem to notice the distress in Christine who has been mentally ravaged by this sequestration on the hill. What is there to do all day, such a fragile being, what can we do with Jonathan, Christine wonders, why are we here so far from everyone else? When can I go back to my university courses? Will life ever be normal again? Jonathan is magnificent but I am white and Jonathan is black. Paris, we'll never go to Paris, like Robert says, he's so unrealistic, more dreams and empty words—in a weary gesture, Christine rocks her child, lifts him to her breast, she is not yet twenty, what will their future bring, she thinks in the immense silence of the forest.

Tomorrow, at dawn, Christine's parents and Robert, they'll all go fishing, she'll be alone at last, thinks Christine, she'll have to make a decision. The following morning, the heat is already suffocating when they leave to go fishing at dawn. Christine begs Robert to leave her alone with the child when he comes to kiss them goodbye; he is so disturbed by Christine's cold attitude, rather than withdrawing as Christine has asked him, he kisses her several times, holds her and Jonathan tight in his arms; they'll only be gone for a few hours, he says, they'll be back at noon. As he leaves the mother and child to walk down to the lake, Robert is seized by sombre premonitions; reluctant to open the door, he turns to gaze at them sadly. He says: "Try to sleep, Christine, we all think you need to rest... You must recover completely before we leave for Paris..."

Anthony's boat glides over the water, it's already so hot, Robert's forehead is burning. "They're going to sleep," Robert says to Charles. "Jonathan and Christine need to rest."

In Anthony's cottage on the hill, Christine puts her child to sleep. They are sleeping. Christine and Jonathan will never awaken. The newspapers will speak of a misfortune, "a depressed young woman kills herself along with her child," they'll say.

# Notebook 43

*For several days* I've been trying to find a musical passage for my novel; the silhouettes of those who will become Uncle Cornelius, Carlos, Venus, hover around me in the heat; this music must be funereal but not sad, a pious yet serene meditation, music where the exaltation of life is carried by an urge to dance, it will be the music of black funerals that I'll hear with John Hersey on Windsor Lane. Thanksgiving Day dinner will end amidst the flowers in David's garden on Elizabeth Street; we are all about to leave, the day is white, very pale, in keeping with the drowsy sensation, the sudden afternoon torpor as we all go home to our rooms to work until evening. We're walking slowly toward the narrow opening of Windsor Street when John tells us to follow him, his finger raised toward the music filling the air: "Listen," he says, and John Malcolm, Rollie, Jimmy, several of his friends are there at his side, contemplating the street procession, standing on the sidewalks where there is no shade; this music, its pomp, with the booming voice of the solo saxophone that seems to fill the heavy air, its weariness throbbing in the beat of the drumsticks, overwhelms John and me at the same time. We'll attempt to retrace it, for a long time the sound will haunt us and in our books, it will disappear, become almost inaudible in the density of the written lines, or beneath the pounding of Carlos' footsteps when the patrol cars hunt him down in the night. How did it sound on that particular day, we'll sometimes try to remember, John and I, what sombre sadness and resignation gave birth to this music, which was also a cantata in praise of God? But a broken cantata, subdued; the poignant melody of the wandering jazz band, during the funeral procession on Windsor Lane that gathered us together in the street for a ceremony which is also a leave-taking.

It's a pale summer day when they converge around John Hersey again in Martha's Vineyard, the island in Massachusetts where John lived with his family for many years, he who enjoyed living in one insular country after another, with his wife Barbara at his side, both of them studious and peaceful, respectful of one another, so discreet they prefer to go unnoticed even in their kind hospitality—this time, on Martha's Vineyard, it's Barbara who says to those who have come to pay homage to her husband: "Listen to that music." They are there, as they were yesterday on the sun-drenched sidewalks of Windsor Lane, listening to the slow-motion march of black funerals, they have come from all over the country, John Malcolm Brinnin, James Merrill, Richard and Charlee Wilbur, David Jackson, Margie Land, and many others, Dr. Gary Montsdeoka, David Wolkowsky, musicians, journalists, the director of the repertory theatre at Harvard University; John belonged to the diversity of this spiritual community, they came from afar to celebrate the author of so many important and human works, the man who was their friend and whose ashes now rest in a garden in the sun; and each woman, each man, head bowed over the secret of his or her destiny, thinks about how little time is left, for without

John the future suddenly seems foreshortened; how could he depart so quickly, they wonder, he didn't even have time to finish his book; just days ago, he was telling me about it, all the portraits, all the characters he was sketching with the exquisite strokes of his style, with the discretion of soul that distinguished him from the other writers of his generation, the elegance of mind, like that of Oriental painters whose brushes are so fine; it is the elder of our community of writers who is departing, who will be next, they think, could it be him, her or me? Every woman, every man Barbara invited to Martha's Vineyard, in a private garden where the birds are singing, where John and Barbara's grandchildren are running through the trees in their formal clothes, rumpled and mussed by the heat—even the knot on their grandson Eric's tie has slipped down over his white shirt, and beneath the straight hair that hides his eyes, Eric purses his lips, as if pouting with pain—everyone is listening to this music which not so long ago, John, hurrying toward Windsor Lane in the sun so bright it bleached the cobblestones, told them to listen to, as if he had said, in a polite confession to each and every one of us: "My friends, listen carefully to this music... for soon this meditation that is pious but not lugubrious, these dancing sounds, this celebration of a passing farewell, will be for me..."

# Notebook 44

*A homeless man*, a satchel slung over his shoulder, comes into the Harbor Lights Bar at the hour when the fishermen return to the port in their boats which seem to slice the water with their wakes, almost silently, in the light of the sun setting over the Atlantic. From the table where I'm writing by the open window, I can see the stranger become agitated as tells his story to a group of fishermen standing with him at the bar. He's come back from far away, he says, like many of the American soldiers reported missing in action after the Vietnam War. His country, the army are still looking for him, he says, he's suffering from amnesia, he caught a deadly fever while wandering through some tropical country, he doesn't even know how he landed in this port, tomorrow he'll be on his way again, it was a very dirty war, he says, those who were sent, like him, never really returned; if they did come back, aren't they morally absent from life even when their lives seem to have been redeemed, so long after those years of massacre? Those soldiers who dropped bombs on the villages, even when they've become comfortable husbands and fathers, orderly, dutiful men, cannot be trusted, he says.

He talks like this for quite a while, with the detachment that drunkenness suddenly brings, but the others are not listening. He is one of Jack's nomad brothers; Jack would have this man's face, he would have caught the same fever in the jungle, he'd have the same eyes distraught with guilt, people would be searching for him too, a conscientious objector, he would still be devastated by the bloody scenes he would have witnessed, in that other life nobody seems to remember today. "What do you expect," says one of the fishermen, "that was a long time ago. You have to learn to forget."

Yet the homeless man who buys his clothes in army surplus stores has preserved the look of the soldier he was, his hair once wavy, like Jack's hair pulled back in a ponytail, has been cut, now his face is austere, his skull bare, his manners nervous, almost aggressive, his body is agile, but under his khaki-coloured shirt his muscles twitch, he looks as if he's still in uniform and ready to bolt when the enemy attacks. He says his parents must have forgotten him. "They think I'm dead," he says, "and I am."

Yet his mother, like Jack's mother, years ago in her house on Cape Cod, still waits daily for a letter from her son in danger. Suddenly insolent, he orders the waitress to bring him another beer—the young woman hesitates and suggests that he go home instead. He gets angry, he says bitterly that he lives on the beach, that he takes shelter from the cold in the winter by sleeping in a canoe, under a blanket. The fishermen have docked their boats. They laugh together as they wash down their decks, scooping up in pails the stream of silvery fish streaked with red splotches that slip through the holes in the nets. The homeless man doesn't like this serene time of day when everyone admires the soft, lovely sky, satisfied with the day's work; these fishermen and their jovial mood irritate him. He looks around suspiciously, he feels as if someone is watching him from the shadows. They'll take him to trial, he'll be judged; in his demented fear, he mimes the gesture of aiming his gun, then calms down. No one can recognize him here.

The images of hell are foggy in his memory. The drowsiness that overtakes his mind when he drinks is like the euphoria he used to feel when he smoked opium by the docks in Saigon. He stands up from the barstool where he was sitting and walks toward the sea, in the high wind that makes the windowpanes rattle; the man shivers when he thinks about the cold that could seize him in the night while he sleeps on the beach, and what if one of those kids comes tonight to steal his blanket?

Standing near the door, he can hear the water lapping at the pilings beneath the deck—tomorrow at dawn he'll find refuge in a boat that will take him away, far from this infernal port, he thinks, where young girls, young women, murdered and raped, appear to him in the midst of the waves—the malaria, the fever must have affected his brain. Why does shame still torment him after so many years? He was just another soldier obeying the laws of war and its slaughter. But every day, by the sea, especially at nighttime, even though he's been suffering from acute amnesia recently, he can hear the tortured voices of the young girls, the young women who cry: "Remember me, you took my life."

# Notebook 45

*hen I see Robert again* at a writers' meeting in Boston, among some hundred writers and poets who have travelled from all over North America, it is shortly before his departure for Paris where he'll join the black writers Richard Wright and James Baldwin who have already been living in exile for several years. Robert has published his fifth novel, *The Promised Land*, defying the insolence and viciousness of the critics who after his first book predicted that Robert would stop writing. As in the past, he runs his fingers through his thick hair, walks over and kisses me, but everything in his attitude is tense, angry, he never chose "the peace of compromise," the peace of the non-violent Blacks, the watered-down expression of their struggle, he says, for he has never shared the faith in humanity, in mankind's progress in the years to come that is Barbara's ardent belief; for him, this world corrupted by spilled blood—he evokes the painful memory of Martin Luther King's assassination, then Malcolm X—this world is irremediably lost. In the soft lamplight of the hotel restaurant where we go for dinner, people no longer stare at us the way they did in that restaurant in the dunes by the sea; here, in this world of intellectuals, no one notices us, and Robert is struck by this invisibility. "I'm undoubtedly the only black writer at this colloquium and nobody seems to notice my presence," he remarks with a dazzling but tortured smile, "I've often written about the invisibility of my race…" And yet, I think, as I listen to Robert, how can one help but notice this young man at the peak of his strength and even of his unhappiness, how can one fail to recognize that he is already, though not yet thirty, an important witness of black America like his elders, Baldwin and Richard Wright? Twenty years later, in 1986, when appointed to the Legion of Honour in France, James Baldwin will also be one of these invisible and misunderstood writers, as was Robert—in his own country, no American publisher will accompany him to France for the Legion of Honour reception, the New York literary world will never award him the Pulitzer Prize or the National Book Award. Robert seems to anticipate these injustices for himself, with a violent gesture, he slams his book on the table between us. "I wrote it thinking of Jane, for her," he says, "not for those publishers who train us black writers like pet dogs, giving us the occasional treat, saying: don't ask for more, keep your mouth shut, while we make a fortune off your secret misery… or the misery of people of your race…" Robert's voice softens when he tells me he took flowers to Jane's grave. Jane, Christine, Jonathan are all sleeping together in the secluded cemetery in Truro, near the dunes, where one can hear the nearby ocean roar. Robert will be leaving the country alone, he'll start a new life. "Adding more ashes to ashes… but what do I have to lose?" His long slender hand, with the pale nails, rests on the shiny cover of his book— despite his pain, Robert's impatient fingers caress this book with pride. "That's what my book is about, the promised land, the story of my life betrayed in the promised land. It's Cape Cod, all of us… the hatred orchestrated over the colour of my skin. The envy, the jealousy of this one or that one. Jane's maternal love that was my salvation, my leaving the streets of Harlem at sixteen, Harlem where, like Baldwin, I've never been able to return... prostitution in the streets of New York when everyone had abandoned me... Gilberte's voluntary or involuntary calumny—innocence gets you nowhere in life... I've received no revelations, except for anger and hatred. One has to have the courage to hate, otherwise how could I write? And don't I have to write to defend the memory of those who died because of me, Jane, Christine, Jonathan?"

But when Robert interrupts the stream of his confidences— for it's another book he's writing, with his words, the tumultuous song of his voice—the dream of the promised land is still with us, there's the summer sky over the beach, a painter sitting on a rock painting the changing sky, its moody subtlety, our lives on the Atlantic coast, all that floods our memory in these few words, "Cape Cod for me, a poor boy from Harlem, was the promised land... Harvard, all the rest, and look what they did to me... They tried to destroy me... but it was the promised land... The land we'll never be allowed to enter, us Blacks..." Who is listening to Robert in this restaurant in the elegant Boston hotel where American writers and intellectuals have gathered? The two of us are alone and never has Robert been more invisible; his book, that he placed on the table with such rage, *The Promised Land*, this immobile object with its shiny cover, is a beneficially dangerous product, as explosive as a bomb, but people have yet to hear its detonation.

# Notebook 46

*She painted the red chair* facing the ocean; when she comes to Wellfleet in the fall, it's with her watercolours, to paint the view from her room on the bay side—she likes how the window frames the shoreline, and the shading of light on the sandy hills. Several of these painters have already left these shores—Leonid, Frances, Henry Poor. Diana quietly pursues the execution of this work sent to her by fate and those who departed before her; she rises every day at six, climbs the narrow staircase to her studio in her early 19th century house, in this refuge in the stern forests of Vermont, in Brattleboro. At over eighty, she draws and paints with the steady hand that could be the hand of Fra Angelico painting a fresco in his convent in Fiesole. The figures that come to life beneath Diana's brush are not those of *Christ aux outrages* or *The Crowning of the Virgin*, but like the Italian painter, she lives and expresses her artistic skill with monastic simplicity, with so little tolerance for modern life and its conspiracy against silence that she never sees the images transmitted by television, not even to while away the hours in the evening. Mornings, when she awakes, in her spacious kitchen, Juliette, Frances' cocker spaniel, and Fred, her springer spaniel, are no longer waiting for her by the wood stove; yet it seems as if these creatures she once adored will bound toward her in the fluid movement of their paws raised in a joyful leap, and that she'll open the door and watch them race into the snow, but when she rises, she is greeted only by the snowy dawn and woods as far as the eye can see, it's already time to start working, she thinks as she drinks her coffee, gazing at this stubborn landscape whose colour she will have to heighten, even if the light does remain dull for a long time in this colourless season. No voices, no dogs barking in the old kitchen; Diana listens to the first news of the day on the radio, she wishes she were deaf to the sinister echoes she hears but the rumble of the world will never cease, she thinks, nothing has really changed since the days of World War II, when fleeing that era of persecution and dreadful events, she survived with Frances in a village near Vence, raising rabbits; no one is any more sheltered in this world today than she was at the time, in the Maritime Alps, always fearing some betrayal, but one day in Vence there was a chapel conceived and decorated by Matisse; who would have believed in such a miracle after Hitlerism had taken over Europe, and didn't this miracle of art prove the permanence, the eternity of art in this world? One still admires with the same wonder paintings by Piero della Francesca, one of the masters, along with Fra Angelico, who inspire Diana, the austerity of the Italian painters is hers, every superfluous stroke of the pen or pencil would be false, unnecessarily heavy; this is how we should live, she thinks with the same rigour, the same rejection of any influence that might make us stray from the chosen path. The studio where she paints has the white walls of a cell, no one ever enters, no discordant sound either, no music; later in the day she'll listen to a Mozart concerto, after teatime at four o'clock, before she resumes her domestic chores: cutting wood, filing papers. Then the books, written in Italian, in German, in French, in English; Diana applies to her reading the same rules of integrity and strict concentration that dictate her daily routine, reading this way several hours a day, her head held high above the pages of the book, without glasses.

When she entertains friends, they are polite, distinguished, sometimes they are painters; Laetitia who comes from Capri every year to see Diana, Laetitia whose painting is overflowing and sensual, it's the magic of this contrast that attracts Diana, it's the same Italian light but a fiery light, the volcanic light of the Mediterranean islands that Laetitia paints while Diana, in her private contemplation of the canvas on her easel, retains only the sober tones. Hence the landscape of Sicily to which she returns in her studio, the drawing of a house with a low roof completely isolated, humble, in the hollow of the plains where wheat and grape vines grow, this house that resembles Diana, with her fierce courage, the almost religious fervour of her desire for solitude. I, too, know, since the fall of 1963, the fall when the tree with the gnarled trunk was painted, drawn, with all the details of its branches exposed to the icy climate, I know Diana's attentiveness to her friends, those who like Laetitia, Mary, John, Franny and myself, pass through her secluded life, I can feel this hand of Fra Angelico, of Piero della Francesca come to rest on my shoulder, then quickly withdraw, and one can never know, I think, when visiting these secret regions of a being, these always brief, reverent visits, what is happening beneath the calm features of the *Crowned Virgin* or the *Outraged Christ*, yet an eternal dignity reposes there; in these regions of the heart, the wounds have been healed, consoled, peace reigns.

Diana listens to the murmur of voices on the radio, these noises that offend her, shatter her, every morning at six o'clock, this murmuring in the dark; then comes the comforting glow of morning, its rosy reflection on the snow, she should let the dogs out, but they are no longer there; it would be time to serve Laetitia breakfast in her room, but she had to leave early this year to join her son in Rome. As she does every morning, at exactly the same time, Diana goes upstairs to her studio; the watercolour of Sicily is there, on the easel, unfinished yet perfect and Diana thinks she doesn't have a second to lose, not an idle second, she must, in her contemplative execution, free the painting of anything superfluous; at last she is alone, she thinks, within the white walls of her cell, and this is a peace no one can disturb.

# Notebook 47

*He bursts like a gust of wind,* one day in the late seventies, into the compartment of the train from Quimper to Paris; where is he going from there, he still has no idea, he'll jump on board the next train to Amsterdam, if he feels the urge; he has already crisscrossed every city in Europe more than once, travelled across Siberia by train—he has the conventional looks of a West Point cadet, a somewhat square head on powerful shoulders, his strength, his build are those of a dreamy giant. After tripping over the four passengers in the compartment with his feet clad in heavy boots covered with mud, he comes to sit across from me and the book I'm reading slips from my hands when these horrible feet come to rest on my seat. Not bothering with useless niceties, David says with a broad smile, "I have to put my feet somewhere, how are you?" He writes hastily with his left hand on a pad of paper, his handwriting is tangled and unruly, I'm incredulous when he tells me he's a writer, nor does he believe me when I say that I too have written several books, that I'll be having breakfast today with my publisher, Robert Laffont, in Paris; he says with the smile that reveals the small gap between his front teeth: "It's amazing that we're both in the same train, the same compartment, but that's how life is, life is unfailingly marvelous..." David tells me that to preserve the freedom to write, he has worked at every trade: he's been a soldier in Korea, he's sounded the alarm for fire-fighters in the burning forests of Santa Barbara on the Pacific Coast, he fell in love with science in Zurich, in the lab where Ruth, his wife, is a researcher, highly thought of in European and American universities, for her studies in molecular genetics. One day I'll go with David to this lab in Zurich to see Ruth bending with meticulous concentration over the fate of fruit flies—we'll also go together to the Alps where David proves to be an indefatigable walker and a connoisseur of the Alpine range—we will refuse, however, Ruth and I, when David suggests that we spend the night on a bed of ice, in one of those caves he knows by name, under the transparent cupola of the glaciers. In the chalet where we choose to sleep, David opens the windows wide onto the starry night, we shiver with cold, our faces bathed in the icy breath that blows in off the mountains. Before resuming our steep climb the following morning, David cooks some sausages over a fire of twigs he unburies in just seconds on these snowy summits towering over Europe. But mostly David writes, he writes everywhere, even while he talks, managing in several languages, when he discusses with inexhaustible knowledge the most diverse subjects, his notepad is covered with frenetic signs written with the left hand—I'm afraid I'll never see him again when we part that day at Montparnasse station, but a month later he joins me in Brittany, it's old Jeanne who comes running to tell me in her gravelly voice: "There's a man who spent the night in the field with the sheep and he says he knows you..." and there's David headed calmly toward me, through the field where Willy and Georgie, the pet sheep, follow close on his heels, their horned foreheads ready to charge our legs and the fence posts. Ten years later, in Québec, I'll find him one morning in the barn in Kingsbury, hay in his hair; he'll simply say: "I was passing through Richmond by train so I decided to stop by and give you my manuscript. It's the sixtieth manuscript I've finished..." David Steward is a genius neglected by publishers, an avant-garde writer whose mind captures like radar the fluidity and rapidity of the events that we are living without understanding them. David writes everything down on his notepad and reading these notes, transcended by the art of the poet, can seem as familiar as reading the morning newspaper, because we know what the weather is like, which catastrophes, which decimations have shaken our world, in David's direct, immediate words, with their accelerated pace, breathing and racing as fast as our lives, the everchanging tale of our contemporary world becomes an epic poem, vast and open to everything that can transpire from one hour to the next, for David's magnetic mind seems to retain everything that happens, from the miracles of technology to the crumbling of societies, everything is present, the earth quakes, we can hear the rumble, but the man whose antennae can already perceive the vibrations of the 21st century believes that all this cacophony is a prelude to new resurrections, prodigious births. Like Gardner, whose music was considered noisy by people unable to hear it at the time, David captures new sounds in this journey through his times, and like Gardner, his music is not understood. But blessed with such great creative vitality, David refuses to be discouraged by the publishers who turn down his novels. Over the years, many of his poems and short stories are published in literary reviews all over the United States. He also has excerpts from his manuscripts reproduced and mails them to friends everywhere in the world, and slowly but surely his writing reaches a growing circle of readers. He will always write, wherever he is, in buses, trains or in the plane on his way to visit his brother Peter in Paris, or in Leningrad where he'll travel alone, writing in a train station, his notepad on his lap, in the merciless upheaval of our revolutions, our wars, from one country to another or alone facing the green glow of his computer, no heavier than a box of chocolates, he writes, in his room in Princeton close to the lab, where, as he did in Zurich, he marvels at Ruth's discoveries and hails her as a future Nobel Prize winner, a woman laureat at last, for David is also a staunch feminist, as well as a solitary prophet, this Walt Whitman from the land of America today.

# Notebook 48

*All three of them belong* to the same dazzling family, Bessie Breuer, novelist and playwright, Henry Poor, painter, ceramist, and Annie, Anne Poor, their daughter who still paints and exhibits her remarkable paintings in New York galleries or in private collections, which also include Henry Poor's work, throughout the United States. Annie is the only living member of this astonishing and solid trio that still seems as indivisible to me today as it did yesterday, in Bessie's house in the hills of Truro in the summertime or in the studio on the farm that belonged to Annie, always veiled in the mists of Maine, a studio I can still see lit by an oil lamp when night falls and we are all gathered in a dark room, arranged like one of Van Gogh's compositions, with the reflections of yellow light on our foreheads, one of Henry's colourful bowls full of fruit on a sideboard, one of Annie's drawings, often a sketch for a portrait, drying on a wall. In Truro, it's Bessie who exerts her fascination on young writers like Robert and me—the woman who wrote *Memory of Love*, a first novel which, when it was published in 1935, Carson McCullers called "a little masterpiece," and Clifton Fadiman, "a classic," she who seduces us as much by the depth of her books as by her personality, her complex, difficult character. Like every true writer, Bessie often seems to be struggling with herself, fighting the demons who possess her, like the Russian writers to whom she is often compared, Chekhov, Turgenev. For Bessie is both kind and violent, gentle and fierce, her words can pierce us like darts, but in her gruff indulgence she also seems to be telling us: "Learn to defend yourselves in life... be strong..." and we listen to her with an uneasy respect. When I first meet her, in 1964, Bessie has finally consented, with the moral support of Barbara who is urging her to take up writing again, to revise her play *Sundown Beach*, first directed by Elia Kazan in 1948 in an Actors Studio production, but although she is writing and rewriting this play that depicts so well the moral and mental breakdown of ex-servicemen during the post-war years, what Kay Boyle, in her preface to the play published by Grindstone Press in 1973, refers to as "the emptiness of the unhappy victory" in 1945, Bessie no longer seems to enjoy writing as she once did. She fears she has lost— in the bitterness of waiting, during the painful silence which followed the publication of her short stories, after the resounding success of her first book—her spontaneity, her freshness; the drama of these disillusioned characters sentenced by the end of the war to poverty and restlessness, isn't it her own drama, she asks? With the stubbornness which can often be helpful to her friends, Barbara keeps repeating that *Sundown Beach* must be staged in this decade of the sixties plagued by cynical violence, isn't the sincerity of this play just what the young militants are waiting for? Barbara is the one who will rid Bessie of her doubts and hesitation—*Sundown Beach* will open in a new production directed by Salem Ludwig, in New York, on May 12, 1964, and Bessie's Chekhovian characters will come to life again, but ever so briefly, for the country, far from sharing the pacifist beliefs of

Bessie and her writer friends, is only concerned with war, and thus the play will meet with the undeserved fate of being virtually forgotten.

Then come the pernicious years of sickness, the lively woman who had been such a subtle raconteur, the one who took us behind the scenes in the world of New York actors, into the homes of her writer friends, the friend of Carson McCullers, of Elia Kazan, has aged and suddenly falls silent; she lives with Annie in the house Henry built in New City, a true work of art, the home and workplace of the painter and ceramist, Henry Poor. It's a Chagalian house built rather to live in not to die in; Bessie now lives there confined to a single room, consumed by the pain in her throat, her voice so weak she has to use a bell to call Annie. This is how I'll hear her for the last time, in that room in New City, and listening to the sound of that bell saying goodbye, the sound of the bell held defiantly in the hand of a dying woman, I'll feel as if I can hear all the paintings in the house vibrate in their frames, like stained glass windows in a cathedral. It's there in that bed, that room of the final farewell, that Annie painted her mother as she saw her then, a frail yet strong mother, her gaze subdued by so much suffering and silent withdrawal— while her body, her head have shrunk with pain, as if they'd been reduced to the dimensions of a bird fallen from its nest, a glow of open-hearted fierceness still dwells in her eyes, her gaze is a restless flame that shines in the ruins of her destroyed body, and this flame is Annie's soul, I thought as I looked at the painting in a New York gallery; it is the palpable and lasting bond between mother and daughter, between Bessie and all of us who knew her and read her books. And yet this trio remains indivisible— in the hills of Truro, I can still see Annie showing her niece

Anna (who will also become a painter and sculptor) how to paint the apple tree, the cherry tree, with a single stroke of her pencil or pen, Bessie is taking a walk, her manuscript in her hand; no, she won't take up writing again, she says to Henry who is working in the garden, she hates writing, she's in a dreadful mood, but nevertheless she closes the door to the house behind her and disappears till evening. Bessie writes for Barbara, if only to please this noble and tender woman who demands so much honesty from her, this woman she finds so unbearable at this very moment, Bessie writes for Barbara and, with a sense of urgency, she revises *Sundown Beach*. Later, over a delicious meal prepared by Henry, Bessie is more cheerful, her grandchildren are there, Anna, her cats and her rabbits; each of the children has done a drawing, a watercolour; content with her day navigating the hazardous shoals of words, Bessie tells her family, her friends, in a moment of satisfaction still full of doubt: "Maybe Barbara was right to insist that I rewrite *Sundown Beach*."

# Notebook 49

*He too is there*, alone on the island, the wild island, unspoiled, the island without sanitation or drinking water in this part of the world forgotten by everyone, that Thomas Sanchez will soon transform into the island of *Mile Zero*, the novel which Thomas had undoubtedly begun to sketch and shape back in those distant years. I can see him reading at eleven in the morning, facing the sea, smoothing his mustache beneath his straw hat—sometimes he is all pensive immobility, his shoulders leaning against the back of his wooden chair, a roomy chair in which he seems so comfortable, stretching his robust body, leaning over to take off his sandals and watch his bare feet sink into the warm sand. I imagine that like me he lives in an attic room on Eaton Street where his feet brush cockroaches when he gets up in the morning, or where, scowling like Thomas, he bangs his soul against the four walls as he writes, pacing back and forth. It's better not to run into Thomas at eleven o'clock when he's striding through the town in a fog that refuses to lift, it's better not to speak to him when he's hiding beneath his football cap, but the writer whose face is tanned by the sun that sparkles through his straw hat, an insomniac like Thomas, as I'll learn when I read his *Memoirs* at the library, is open and friendly, his voice is jovial when he asks a waiter who is walking dreamily with his tray at the edge of the waves, the gentle, regular waves of foggy mornings, to bring him some strawberries for breakfast, and perhaps a martini to wake him up as well. It's Stella, a palmreader at the restaurant Chez Claire, who first mentions him to me: "Tennessee and Rose are my cousins," says Stella, absorbed in her study of the lines of my hand, about to retrieve me from the abyss with her dazzling art of divination. "If you stay with us here in the sea air," she says as she feels my fingertips and scans the lines of my palm, my wrist, "you'll be cured of the aftermath of this pulmonary congestion... And you'll get a lot of writing done. Come visit me at home, I'll show you some paintings by Tennessee and his sister Rose. I've often taken care of her. She;s a charming woman who has inspired many characters in Tennessee's plays. Her view of the world is different from ours. That's why she needs to be protected, she's blessed... a creature blessed by God but misunderstood by us. A flower imprisoned in a greenhouse, not because it's poisonous but because it would die if exposed to our poisons. I often visit her in her rest home, sometimes I invite her to come out with me... and that's when I really discover her poetry, her secret poetry." In Stella's bare home, there is a single room and paintings cover the only wall; Stella seems to live outside on her balcony, and she simply has to walk down the street to Chez Claire, her dog Sugar under her arm, but Sugar is getting old, his black button eyes are sad, his pink tongue lolling, and he trails behind his mistress, bewildered, bobbing his head. In the sun-filled room, Tennessee Williams' paintings, those of his sister Rose and Stella's own invite me into a strange, bewitching world. I think of the man I saw at The Sands beach reading in the morning, alone, facing the sea, he is the one who painted these serene nudes, the intoxicating sensuality of these pastels, in his landscapes flooded with blue water that sings; the obsessive harassment that writing exercises on every writer has disappeared from these paintings, the light is intense, blue or white with fog as it was this morning on the beach where the author of these paintings was relaxing, barefoot in the sand surrounded by gulls. Back in the room haunted by his ghosts, *The Inner Room*, the room where all the doors are closed of which the great poet James Merrill speaks, the man who recovers here from his nights of despondency and turmoil will soon be confronted with the ever so fragile ghost of the woman who was Rose, shunted aside, the true character of *The Glass Menagerie*, whom the muses in their panic abandoned.

Rose, whose path was that of a poet, even during her confinement for a convalescence that would last her entire life—Stella stays close to Rose, through her brother's paintings, his manuscripts, his drawings. Is it Stella or Rose who painted the canvas entitled "Tonight Something Will Happen"? The two cousins share such intense affinities they both seem to penetrate the same invisible world, they shake those glass paperweights where storms rise and winds blow. A bird painted by Stella is larger than life because it is larger than life in reality, the island is a miniature expanse of water, and when Stella paints her sun, it's Provence that floods the painting, for that is how it is, she says, the bird is immense compared to the eye that beholds it, so huge it spills over the rigid edges of the painting and we can see the immensity of its expectation as its outstretched wings embrace the sky. In Rose's painting, "Tonight Something Will Happen," a table awaits guests in a garden: is it being set or cleared? The spoons, the knives are topsy turvy on the red tablecloth, there are flowers, if those *are* flowers, but the vase has been placed beside the flowers, in the background, a woman is waiting for her guests, her dress might be black or dark red, the balance between the objects and the figure is distorted, the subject of the painting is adrift on its sea of iridescent colour, "tonight something will happen." A woman is waiting for visitors, perhaps they have come, but suddenly everyone is gone. Rose, like Stella on her stage at Chez Claire, guessed, had a presentiment of everything that would happen after a long evening of festivities on the white terrace where the laughter of young people could be heard, they were all invited to the banquet but have departed, there's no sense in setting the table now, the forgotten flowers would wilt in their vases, a woman is waiting, in the empty dining room in the restaurant, but no one will come, because tonight something has happened.

# Notebook 50

*ortense, Hortense Flexner*. Her name is pronounced, in 1993, by one of her contemporary readers who discovered her work in Marguerite Yourcenar's translation. It's Jean Fougère who mentions her during an interview, and suddenly she has joined us, she has emerged from the silence of the shadowy mountain where, as in her poems, she had to fight "surrounded by angels, but foolishly with a sword against the archaic warrior." She is a tiny, kindly woman with a spontaneous smile, I meet her when she is well along in years, she trots gaily between Mary and me on our way to Marguerite Yourcenar's garden—Hortense wants Madame Yourcenar to read her latest poems, the ones she wrote in there, in there being the residence where the old people are dozing on this sweltering summer afternoon. It's her new home, and Miss Horti, as Mary, who has known her for a long time, calls her, feels that in this particular place she could easily fall during her battle, dropping the "heavy armor" of the knight, but if death is approaching, she also writes, death will be surprised "to find a hand still warm." And it is Miss Horti's lively hand that guides our steps that day, showing us the open road, the road along the sea, far from the sleepy residence among the trees, far too from all those beds where white faces exhaling inaudible sighs emerge from the tidily folded sheets.

In one of her poems about old age, Miss Horti describes those bodies, those faces slumbering in their funereal withdrawal, in the middle of summer, "these furious skeletons so close to their last breath." Perhaps she had had a premonition of this image when she was still young and vigorous in her house in Kentucky where she did most of her writing, adding to her poetry stories for children that were illustrated by Wyncie King. But it's a fairy, an elf who jumps out of Mary's car and runs to the rocks, the beach, the sea; how many endless days will she have to wait before she can see these unfailing landscapes again? Miss Horti says she always wants to escape at nap time, "but in there, it's always nap time, it's so discouraging...." That day, during tea time at Madame Yourcenar's, we'll learn that Miss Horti's works are going to be published in France; Madame Yourcenar, who translated Cavafy's poems in 1958, is not afraid to introduce French readers to Hortense Flexner's work through her respectful translation of the concise world of Miss Horti, a subtle poet like Cavafy, but whose elegiac tone is more reserved, measured; this measure often present in Hortense Flexner's poems, sometimes provides a comparison, a link, as in the poems where "frail is the flower, fierce the seed," "the physical eye though slim can record ample things forever," or "agony that shall fill him like a cup," and of that full cup, she says "each being must measure what it holds." The critic Laurie Lee writes that these poems "fall like drops of water, each with its own crystalline and pure weight, this writing is rigorous and precise, it has a stark transparency, the world perceived in its minuteness often casts gigantic shadows." But in Madame

Yourcenar's garden, Miss Horti listens modestly to the praise proffered by her imperious friend who is touched by such simplicity, for Miss Horti is sitting on the edge of her chair, her hands on her knees, pulling at the threads of her cotton dress with clumsy fingers; "You are, Hortense, along with Elizabeth Bishop and Marianne Moore who are both discreet women like you, one of the great poets of your generation, and France, Europe should discover you.""But I'll soon be in heaven," says Miss Horti with a mischievous smile. "Now, now," says Madame Yourcenar, "heaven can wait." Tall Grace Frick, who is standing behind Madame Yourcenar's chaise longue, suddenly leans over us painfully, she places her broad hands on her aching kidneys; we can feel how sensitive she is to each of her guests, always ready to help others, although she is already suffering from the serious illness that will carry her away so soon; ignoring the pain, she walks with difficulty to the kitchen and returns with hot, fragrant rolls: "These are for you, Hortense," says Miss Frick. "I know how much you like my rolls. Of course heaven can wait. There are enough people there already, don't you agree, Hortense?"

Shortly after that charming afternoon with Madame Yourcenar and Miss Frick, Miss Horti died in her native Kentucky, but here was undoubtedly an ardent glow that has never ceased to burn. "I believe in the industrious labour of death which is done proudly," she had written not long before then. "My spirit is in dark defeat. A famished fly gnaws at me, I chase it away but it takes the shape of my thoughts." I hope as I read these lines that Miss Horti, whose hand was still warm in the frozen grasp of death, was spared feeling, experiencing, that grip of cold, she who so loved warmth, for whom cold meant the numbness of eternal sleep, "bound to a branch in the icy wind." I hope that "the long stride of the sun" reaches her door, that "the cup of agony" held no more than she could bear, a measure of pain, as Hortense Flexner says, "fitted to one's size."

# Notebook 51

*They leave*, they are on the road like Jack and Robert years ago when they drifted to other continents, other shores, searching for a world where there'd be no need to fear the extinction of nations by a horde of armed speculators; now they are empty-handed, the wind in their hair, they can remember the cloud of smoke barely dissipated over the rice paddies of Vietnam, they can still see the columns of fire and blood rising every day over the scorched earth of the Middle East.

They are thirty in 1990 when they arrive with their dog Spirit in their rickety car, the carcass of a grey Chevrolet, with license plates that proclaim in white letters: "Live free or die." They are my friends Scott Kirby and Michelle Clauson who have given up their family fortune for an unencumbered life; the air they breathe here is light, diaphanous like the green water where they love to swim (they say the air here is so soft we all swim in its transparency), from this diaphanous air and water they've travelled so far to find, they will emerge, their athletic bodies relaxed after happy exertion, and their souls, renewed and ready for adventure.

The distressing burden of industrial cities will fall from their shoulders, they'll have no desire to conquer, they will simply be the creative inventors of their own lives, poets and musicians, and having turned their backs on a career in politics or business that would have enslaved them in lies, they are free to say and write what they feel, their melodies carry their sombre, lucid words, we're moved by the gentle, almost measured passion in their voices, and the prophetic yearning when they evoke the reality of our times. They were afraid the torrid sun on the beaches would make them drowsy, but suddenly stimulated by the warm air, together they set the sails on the boat they've rented and learn to navigate, slowly but surely conquering the tumultuous currents of the Atlantic.

In the evening, when the light from the lamps on the terrace tables leaps and flickers in the wind, I come to listen to Scott's music. It's to the sound of these fading notes on the guitar, the harmonica, that I write the story of Jack, and of Robert, whose lives now seem woven into the bloody fog of the sixties; Scott's haunting lyrics echo in the dark and the tourist staring absently into space doesn't seem to realize these words are meant for him: "Today I met a man whose suffering was majestic," Scott sings, relaxed on his stool, his legs crossed under the seat, dressed in his beige shorts which, apart from a baseball cap when it's cold, is what he wears for all his concerts on the beach, "he's got his house on Long Island, he's got a mansion in Maine, a majestic yacht on the ocean, but he lives in majestic pain. His heart's never beat in the sunshine, never soaked in the rain, he's got blue blood and gold in his porcelain soul, and he lives in majestic pain."

The man who appears like the still agitated ghost of Jack, the deserter people are searching for in the jungles of Asia and who doesn't know where he'll sleep tonight, shudders with a familiar fear, he pulls his blanket tighter around his shoulders when he feels Scott's melodious, calm voice slice through his soul like a knife. "I've been walking now for thirty years, farther east, farther west, I've been walking alone... farther..." These ballads, as lonely as his own heart, will rock him to sleep in his boat under his blanket drenched with the smell of salt, but it's going to be a long night, maybe he should linger a bit longer near the hotel entrances, his hand extended humbly from beneath his blanket, begging?

The reflections of a round and insolent full moon shine on the red legs of the drifter, beneath his blanket, as he heads for the street, a ravaged silhouette, like Jack in my memory. The same reflections that cast cold circles around the moon illuminate Michelle's face as she stands by the bar, listening to Scott sing. There is a relaxed, friendly look on the young woman's face, beneath her tousled blond hair, but the angelic smile, her shining blue eyes, even her loving gaze turned on Scott, everything in this lively face exudes great vitality, prodigious determination too, and as Scott sings "A little bit farther, farther west, farther east... it must be time to leave again," I hear Michelle say to me: "I'm training with the women's team for the big race (the Whitbread Race), soon I'll be captain... I've already won a few trophies, tomorrow I'll be like Amelia Earhart, Nancy Frank... The sails are set... it's our turn now..."

*Translator's note:*

For the benefit of readers who might wish to compare this translation with the original as published by VLB Éditeur, it is important to note that, at the author's request, the translation is based on the text as it was revised for this publication.